"One of the most common questions I'm asked by readers is
where can they go to see all of the art, architecture,
locations, and symbols described in the book?"

—DAN BROWN

"The answer, I hope, can be found in this book."

—PETER CAINE

WALKING THE
DA VINCI
CODE
IN PARIS

PETER CAINE

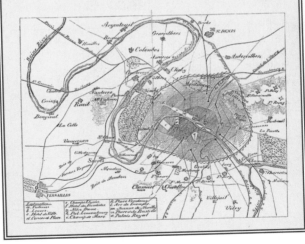

AVALON TRAVEL PUBLISHING

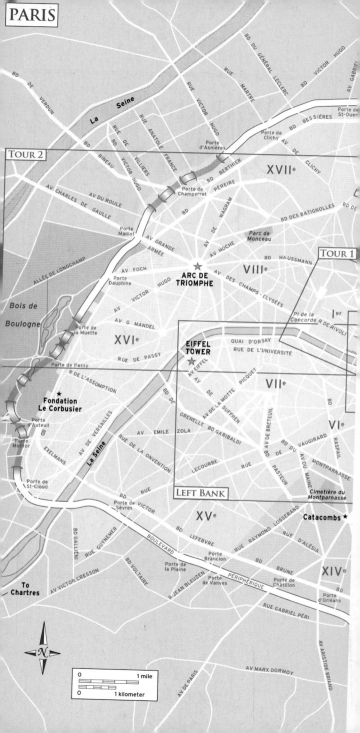

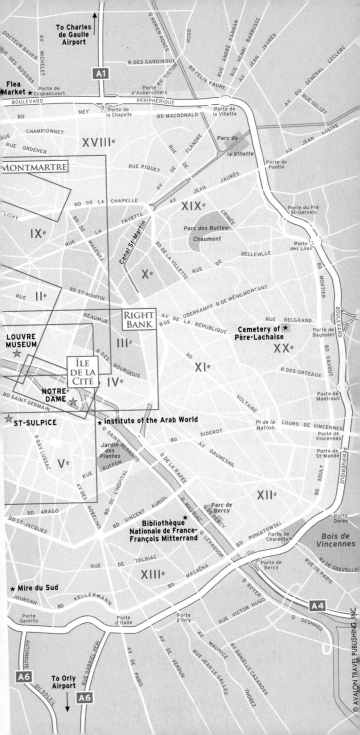

CONTENTS

FOREWORD

This book is for anyone who loves Paris, but especially for those who love to walk its streets with a spirit of discovery. The theme that ties it together is the story told in Dan Brown's best-selling thriller *The Da Vinci Code*. In the book, mystifying codes, secret societies, religious sects, religious controversy, and mysterious monuments are all clues that lead a trail across Paris and beyond—an irresistible quest just waiting to be followed. Whether you have read the book or not, if you are a keen explorer of the city and its many mysteries, this book is for you. This is how it came about:

My wife and I set up Paris Walks more than 10 years ago. As art historians, our purpose was to bring to life 2,000 years of Paris's history, art, and architecture. Literally thousands of people have come on our guided visits to discover the wonders of Paris, its museums, monuments, and ancient historic quarters. Some time ago, like so many others, we began to hear frequent references to a new book, some sort of thriller, set in Paris. In the story, the curator of the Louvre was murdered, while the protagonists departed on a treasure hunt following clues hidden in Leonardo da Vinci's paintings. It's not the kind of book we usually read! As the months went by I was accosted each time I accompanied a group into St-Sulpice Church, and each time I was asked the same questions: "Is there a Rose Line here in the church?" and "Where is the Gnomon?" Eventually my curiosity was aroused enough to acquire the book. I wandered round to the delightful English bookseller Village Voice, tucked away behind St-Sulpice, and bought a copy of *The Da Vinci Code*. I took it home, began to read it, and found, to my astonishment and like millions of others before me, that I just could not put the book down. I was immediately inspired to look at reproductions of the paintings in the book. I simply had to verify the descriptions given by the author. In his introduction, Dan Brown says, "All descriptions of artwork, architecture, documents, and secret rituals in this novel are accurate." But are they? After all, Brown is a novelist and this is a thriller. This gripping novel certainly raises as many questions as it answers!

I soon found that I could not resist the temptation to check all of these curious observations for myself. I set out to look at the paintings closely and to visit the locations. As a trained historian, my first reaction was to go back to the sources and see for myself whether there could be any basis for truth in what Brown was telling his readers. The quest was an intriguing trail that led all over Paris. Our guides quickly became specialists in the subject, researching and leading regular tours on this theme. One of our guides is related to the academic Hugh Schonfield, who wrote *The Passover Plot*, first published in 1967. This book was one of several upon which the controversial subject matter of stories such as *The Da Vinci Code* is based.

As my fascination with researching the sources for *The Da Vinci Code* grew, so did the idea of sharing the results. We soon set up a *Da Vinci Code* Tour of Paris, and it wasn't long before it was spotted by editors Constance de Bartillat and Charles Ficat. Their determination soon transmogrified *The Da Vinci Code* Tour of Paris into the definitive code-seekers' guidebook. As previously stated, many of the ideas in the book are controversial, and many of the so-called facts are troubling; they leave plenty of opening for belief but to really find the answers, the only solution is to go on the trail and decide for yourself.

Brown encrypted a four-part code on the front cover of his book, offering a trip to Paris for the lucky cryptographer who could decode the message—40,000 people returned the answers to him! The book, its secrets, codes, and conspiracy theory have excited the imaginations of millions. So far, more than a dozen books have been written to help the reader decode Dan Brown's book, which is packed full of codes from cover to cover. These books take diverse points of view. Some are tongue-in-cheek, and others defend Christianity, seeing *The Da Vinci Code* as a threat. One such book, recently published in French, disputed, in a mocking tone, every point made by Brown, offering little analysis and no alternative evidence. The best of them take an intelligent look at the questions raised by the novel, examine its contents, and attempt to give a balanced view. This book aims to do this while offering a unique way to visit the city of Paris.

INTRODUCTION

In his novel Dan Brown takes us on a journey across Paris that has its origins in our ancient medieval past. Secret societies, the Knights Templar, the Priory of Sion, Masons, and other mysterious groups used symbols and codes to protect their most precious secrets while passing them on to others. Evidence of this can be found in carvings, sculptures, inscriptions, paintings, and objects in or on the meetinghouses of each. In *The Da Vinci Code*, Brown links these together, sending his hero Langdon on a quest to unravel a code that will lead him to one of the most powerful and carefully kept secrets ever. This guide will take you to those places and reveal some of their hidden secrets.

Even if you have not read *The Da Vinci Code*, you will find you can enjoy this guidebook, and it will initiate you into the mysteries and enigmas of Paris. However, if you have read the book, then as you go you will be able to relive the excitement of the tale as it unfolds and see how some of the intriguing issues raised by Dan Brown relate to the chosen sites and monuments.

This book aims to be a complete manual. It covers the history and background of all the sites mentioned in *The Da Vinci Code*, offering some practical tips as well as containing information about other unusual, mysterious, or

esoteric monuments and meeting places. We will also unravel some of the puzzles and clues that Brown has woven into his text. For example: The rue Haxo really exists, it is not near Roland-Garros as Brown says, there is no number 24, and there is no Depository Bank of Zurich, but . . . Haxo is an anagram of Hoax.

GALLERIES TO GOLGOTHA!

The most dramatic events in the book take place in two places: the magnificent Church of St-Sulpice, and one of the world's most famous museums, the Louvre. This guide will take you on an in-depth tour of both of these monuments, but this trail, like Langdon's quest, will lead all over the city and even take us out into the countryside to the now-famous Château de Villette and the lovely city of Chartres.

St-Sulpice

Dan Brown's novel has done for St-Sulpice what Victor Hugo's *Hunchback of Notre Dame* did for the cathedral of Paris. In the early 19th century the cathedral was in a terribly poor state of repair. As a medieval monument, it was not held in high regard. In this period it was the monuments of the Renaissance that were considered worthy of attention. These were evidence of a Golden Age when at long last men began to live like civilized beings; they were monuments from an age of enlightenment and learning. Medieval Notre-Dame seemed to serve as a reminder of our warriorlike and barbaric past. Hugo's book set both the period and the monument in a completely new light. Literally thousands of visitors came to look at the church again, this time with wonderment at the architectural marvel. The public soon rallied to the cause of preserving what had survived, although it was nearly too late. Medieval windows had been removed to let more light into the church, and the original carved lintel of the central portal had been savagely demolished to allow taller processional banners into the building. The heroic hunchbacked Quasimodo put an end to this destruction.

Hugo's best-selling and wonderfully romantic story, like Brown's, also begins by citing a cryptic inscription. Hugo wrote that he had seen this carved into the ancient stones of the cathedral. Had it been left by a mason, or by an alchemist? Pilgrims and Quasimodo fans have been coming ever since to seek this curious mark and relive the greatest moments of the famous novel. This is now the case with St-Sulpice Church. Visitors come to seek the enigmatic Gnomon beneath which the Priory of Sion's keystone was said to be hidden, and to see where the grisly murder of Sandrine Bieil took place. Hundreds who never came before flock to the church. The church has put articles, clippings, and cuttings everywhere, warning the visiting public that it has no real connection with the history or events as told in a recently published novel.

The Louvre

The current curator of the Louvre is apparently not too pleased at being killed off but is delighted that the museum has found a new crowd of enthusiastic visitors coming to marvel at its magnificent collection of Leonardos. People come to seek coded messages in the *Mona Lisa* and Nicolas Poussin's *Shepherds of Arcadia*. These can be seen with the aid of this guide, but there is also much more to discover, and the aim of this book is to lead you on your way.

CONTROVERSY AND CRITICISM

The Da Vinci Code has sparked huge interest worldwide and has sold millions of copies. A simple web search on Google using *Da Vinci Code* + Dan Brown resulted in 1.27 million hits. But the work has been controversial and the book has been highly criticized from many sides. Religious doctrine, the Holy Grail theory, and the supposed relationship between Mary Magdalene and Christ have all come under heavy criticism. These ideas are not at all new. Nikos Kazantzakis, perhaps best known for writing *Zorba the Greek*, evoked the relationship between Christ and Mary Magdalene in *The Last Temptation of Christ* more than 50 years ago. The Roman Catholic Church banned his book, and the Greek Orthodox Church excommunicated him for this work.

Another of the many criticisms leveled at *The Da Vinci Code* is the errors it apparently makes in describing the topography of Paris. As will be illustrated, there are many reasons why Dan Brown describes the city as he does. It is also important to remember that the book is a novel and that it has been written to entertain, so let your imagination be entertained as you discover Paris and enter into the fun, like the millions of other people who have thoroughly enjoyed this gripping book.

THE BOOK IS DIVIDED INTO EIGHT MAIN CHAPTERS:

The Paving Stones of Paris leads the way through the city to all the locations that are involved in the story.

Beneath the Rose Line is a complete guided tour of St-Sulpice Church.

Under the Pyramids is a guided *Da Vinci Code* tour of the Louvre.

Château Villette and Beyond takes you to the places outside Paris that are vital to the story.

The Keystone: Paris Practicalities provides further ideas for those wishing to take the trail one step further, and it includes some practical information.

The Seven Seals, the first appendix, contains a dictionary of symbols and introduces the main themes and controversies that arise in the book.

Inside the Cryptex, the second appendix, decodes the characters and events in the book, explains the meaning of much of the esoteric vocabulary used by Dan Brown, and deciphers some of the codes.

Isis and the Sacred Feminine, the third appendix, examines the sacred feminine and where to find her in Paris.

In addition, a full **index** makes finding even the lesser-known curiosities easy. We hope you find your quest both enjoyable and rewarding!

THE
PAVING
STONES
OF
PARIS

D AN BROWN has his hero, Robert Langdon, and heroine, Sophie Neveu, traveling across Paris in an extraordinary manner. Critics have railed about the impossibility
of the journeys. Brown has Langdon leaving the Ritz and
going by the Opera to get to the Louvre, which on a map
appears completely impractical. He then has the police driving through the middle of the Tuileries Gardens, which is of
course impossible to do in real life. During the early part of
the story, Sophie and Langdon make an extrordinary getaway from the Louvre. They dash off in Sophie's SmartCar,
they hire a taxi, steal a taxi, and end up at Château Villette in
a stolen armored bank truck. Two choices are available: Take
the critics' view and think "nonsense," or look at this journey
in the light of Brown's book and see what it reveals. Drawing
the route on a map, or following it on Paris buses, begins to
reveal a few interesting clues: As Sophie and Langdon zigzag
their way across the city, they trace a series of triangles, both
blades and chalices. At the Louvre, their circuit forms two
pyramid shapes. They then circle their way along boulevard
Malesherbes, rue de la Pépinière, rue d'Amsterdam, sail past
Montmartre, and head along the avenue de Clichy to the exterior boulevards on their way to the bois de Boulogne. In
doing this they trace a Fibonacci spiral.

TOUR 1:
Langdon Escorted by the Police from the Ritz to the Louvre—The Journey Step by Step

To retrace Langdon's steps, start at 38 rue Cambon (metro Madeleine). The sites and monuments included on the trail are described individually below. This journey can be done by combining walking and the use of city buses. From rue Cambon, head up to the boulevard de la Madeleine on foot, and then follow along to place de l'Opéra (walk or bus 42 or 52). Take the beautiful rue de la Paix to get to place Vendôme and cross the square, continuing in a straight line. When you

the Cathedral of Notre-Dame

come to rue de Rivoli, cross the road to enter the Tuileries Gardens. Continue straight till you come to the central alley, turn left and keep going, walk through the Carrousel Arch, and then turn to the side of the arch and take the entrance to the underground complex of the Louvre. Continue past the ancient archaeological remains of the city wall (dating from 1380). In the distance, you'll see architect I. M. Pei's upside-down pyramid. Keep walking till you come up close, and then, if you feel so inclined, like Langdon, drop to your knees with reverence (or fatigue!).

38 RUE CAMBON

This must be where Langdon began his journey, if he passed the Opera to get to the Louvre. The staff entrance to the Ritz hotel is here, a back door giving onto a quiet street. This is the security entrance that Lady Diana took to leave the hotel as she

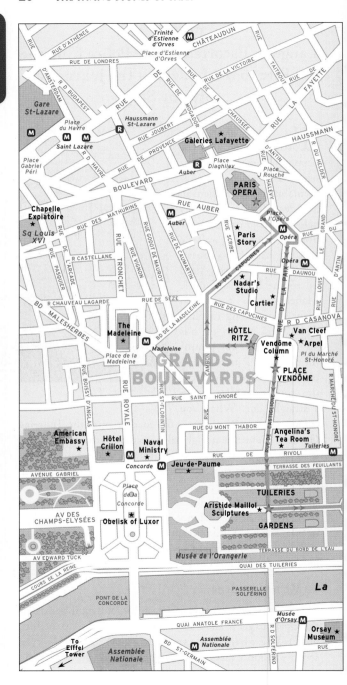

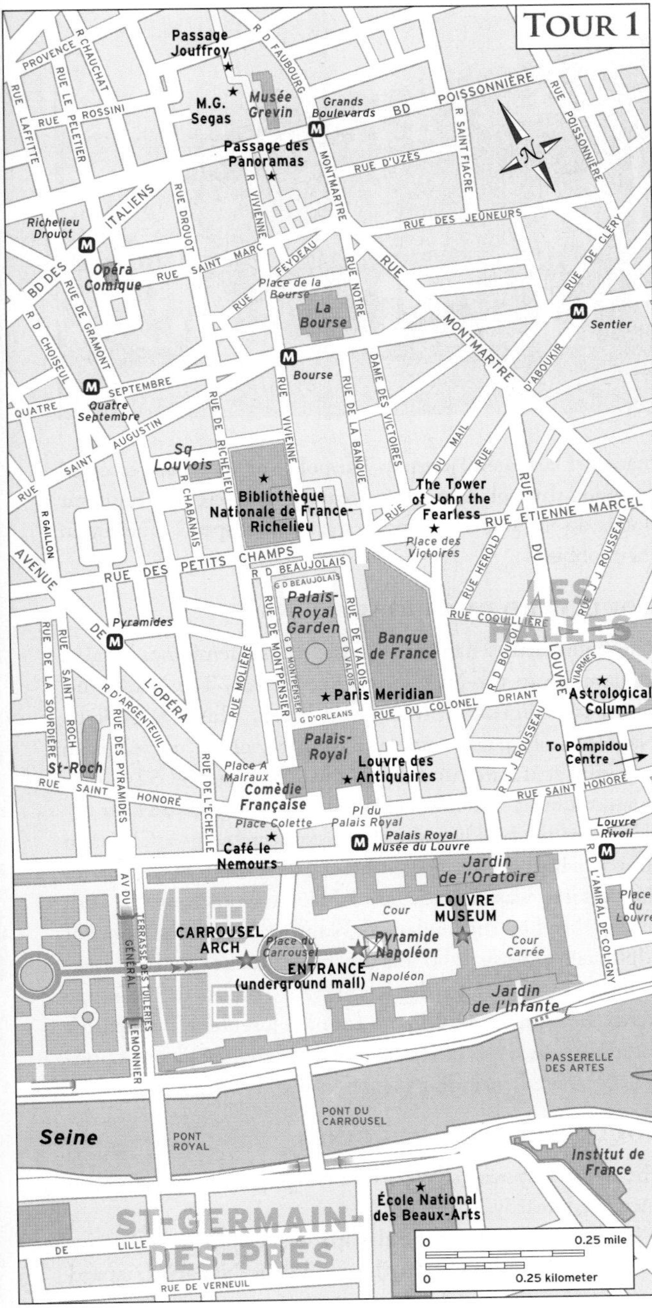

TOUR 1

Passage Jouffroy

M.G. Segas ★   Musée Grevin ★

Grands Boulevards Ⓜ

Passage des Panoramas ★

Richelieu Drouot Ⓜ

Opéra Comique ★

Quatre Septembre Ⓜ

Sq Louvois ★

Bibliothèque Nationale de France-Richelieu ★

The Tower of John the Fearless ★

Place des Victoires

Pyramides Ⓜ

Palais-Royal Garden

Banque de France

LES HALLES

Paris Meridian ★

Astrological Column ★

To Pompidou Centre →

St-Roch

Palais-Royal

Louvre des Antiquaires ★

Comédie Française ★

Café le Nemours ★

Place Colette

Pl du Palais Royal

Palais Royal Musée du Louvre Ⓜ

Louvre Rivoli Ⓜ

Jardin de l'Oratoire

LOUVRE MUSEUM ★

Cour Carrée

Place du Louvre

CARROUSEL ARCH ★

Place du Carrousel

Pyramide Napoléon ★

ENTRANCE (underground mall)

Napoléon

Jardin de l'Infante

PASSERELLE DES ARTES

Seine

PONT ROYAL

PONT DU CARROUSEL

Institut de France

ST-GERMAIN-DES-PRÉS

École National des Beaux-Arts ★

0   0.25 mile
0   0.25 kilometer

© AVALON TRAVEL PUBLISHING, INC.

made her last fateful journey. The police have perhaps escorted Langdon through this exit for reasons of discretion; four-star hotels do not appreciate policemen and suspects loitering in their lobbies.

BOULEVARD DE LA MADELEINE

The boulevard is named after the sacred feminine. It takes its name from the huge templelike church, The Madeleine, which is dedicated to Mary Magdalene. This was built by Napoleon as a pagan temple to the glory of his army. It is an imposing structure surrounded by a colonnade of 52 Corinthian columns, each measuring 20 meters. Napoleon later decided that the building should be consecrated as a Christian church, which was done October 9, 1845, about 80 years after the building was started. Several iconic women of the 19th century lived on the boulevard. Number 15 was the home of Alphonsine Plessis, who was the inspiration for *La Dame aux Camélias* by Alexandre Dumas and *La Traviata* by Guiseppe Verdi. At number 32, Mme Récamier, Josephine Bonaparte's social rival, held her celebrated salon. Here Napoleon's opponents gathered, including one of his own brothers.

BOULEVARD DES CAPUCINES

The name Capucines refers to a congregation of nuns who once lived nearby.

Farther along at 35 boulevard des Capucines, the top floor of the building was the studio of Nadar (Gaspard

Tournachon), a pioneer of photography, whose beautiful portraits are among the most famous in the 19th century. Brown explains that the impressionists painted in the Tuileries Gardens, and the first-ever impressionist exhibition in Paris took place in Nadar's studio in 1874. The paintings were ill received and the artists ridiculed. Nadar invented photography in artificial light, experimenting both in the sewers of Paris and the catacombs.

At number 14, a sign indicates that "the first ever moving pictures animated by a machine invented by the Lumière brothers" were shown here on December 28, 1895 (the name could have been invented by Dan Brown, as *lumière* means "light" in French).

THE PARIS OPERA: A PALACE OF SYMBOLS

The Paris Opera is open to the public for visits. For a full guided tour contact Paris Walks. The building was commissioned by Napoleon III, but unfortunately for him, it was inaugurated only in 1875, after he had died in exile. He was never able to use the magnificent entrance designed so that he could take his carriage right into the building. This sumptuous palace is decorated with an abundance of symbols representing the theater: lyres, masks with grimacing faces, and Apollo, god of the arts and creative energy. The building has always held a strange fascination, especially as it is built on a mysterious source of water that could not be drained away. This water became a lake that links to the sewers in Gaston Leroux's famous story *The Phantom of the Opera*.

☞ *The Paris Opera, place de l'Opéra, 75009, metro Opéra, is open 10am–5pm every day except when closed for special functions; auditorium may be closed for rehearsals.*
☞ *The Sewers Museum (les Egouts) can be visited, place de la Résistance, 75007, at the Left Bank end of Alma Bridge, metro Alma-Marceau (see map, p. 78), open 11am–4pm, closed Thursdays and Fridays.*

RUE DE LA PAIX

The street was originally named after Napoleon, but it was renamed after the Treaty of Paris was signed in 1814. It is world famous for its jewelers; see Cartier at number 9. The fashion house of the Englishman Charles Worth was opened here at number 7 in 1858. Worth, who designed the crinolines of Empress Eugénie, wife of Napoleon III, was the first to show his designs on living models, the first one being his wife.

PLACE VENDÔME

This is one of the five beautiful royal squares in Paris. It was built for Louis XIV, the Sun King. His symbol, the face of Apollo in the center of a sunburst, can be seen on the iron window balustrades. The square is typical of the classical architecture from this period: grand and majestic, with a great feeling for architectural harmony and proportions.

LANGDON—PUTTING ON THE RITZ

At number 15 is the Ritz hotel, where Langdon is staying. Harvard dons obviously have very generous expense allowances or earn a great deal. The Ritz is one of the world's best and certainly most beautiful hotel buildings. Its façade was designed by Jules Hardouin-Mansart, whose family gave its name to the mansard roof. The hotel opened its doors to the public on June 1, 1898, and along with chef Auguste Escoffier, César Ritz soon created a palace of splendor and opulence that attracted a clientele of wealthy socialites. A peep in the guest book reveals: Coco Chanel, who lived here for 30 years, Ernest Hemingway, after whom a cocktail bar is named, F. Scott Fitzgerald, Marcel Proust, Edward VII, Rudolph Valentino, Charlie Chaplin, and Greta Garbo.

The hotel was acquired by Mohamed Al-Fayed in 1979; his son, Dodi, was staying here with Lady Diana when she made her last fateful journey across Paris with him and their driver Henri Paul. Al-Fayed refurbished the hotel and created the Ritz–Escoffier Cookery School.

DIAMONDS ARE A GIRL'S BEST FRIEND

The square is famous for its jewelers. Opposite the Ritz is Van Cleef and Arpels. The shops around the square have given inspiration to a host of Pink Panther–style thieves and several generations of talented crime writers and filmmakers. Look out for Boucheron, Chaumet, Guerlain, Schiaparelli, and Payot.

MEDICINE MAGIC AND MESMERISM

In 1778, Dr. Franz Mesmer opened his consulting room at 16 place Vendôme. A host of illustrious clients, including Marie Antoinette, came here for cures. The sessions began with his clients sitting in a ring around tubs of bubbling chemicals; they held hands in a séancelike manner and then pointed metallic rods in the tubs at an astrological map on the ceiling. The treatment offered was expensive, and Mesmer made a fortune. The success of the cures is doubtful. History records the witty Parisian actress Sophie Arnould taking her sick poodle to see Mesmer. After three days the dog died. "Ah, well," said the actress. "At least he died cured." Needless to say Mesmer was soon out of business.

NAPOLEON, PILLAR OF STRENGTH

In the center of the square stands the Vendôme Column. This was made for Napoleon from 2,000 cannons captured by him at the battle of Austerlitz. It was a copy of Trajan's

Column in Rome, and Napoleon dreamed of having his own mausoleum in its base. The changes made to the statue on top of the column have been emblematic of the city's turbulent past. At first there stood an effigy of the emperor, but this was melted down to make the statue of Henry IV now on the Pont-Neuf. A fleur-de-lis was put in its place but soon changed for Napoleon more simply dressed in his military great-coat. This statue displeased Napoleon III, who replaced it with his uncle and predecessor dressed as an emperor once more. On May 16, 1871, the members of the Commune pulled the column down. The National Assembly decided to reconstruct it in 1872, and it built the column that can be seen today.

RUE CASTIGLIONE AND AN ECCENTRIC COUNTESS

The road is named after another Napoleonic battle, but it was also lived on by the countess of Castiglione, onetime mistress to Napoleon III. The Imperial balls were her favorite pastime. She attended them in extravagant gowns, and guests would stand on chairs to admire her as she entered.

LANGDON SPIES THE EIFFEL TOWER

The 1,000 feet of the Iron Lady have the Harvard symbologist reflecting on the nature of the French. Langdon sees the tower as a phallic symbol. He says the French are renowned for small and insecure leaders, including Pepin the Short and Napoleon. Pepin is the king who bridges the gap between the Merovingian and Carolingian dynasties. The Eiffel Tower appears to have a quasimystical appeal—literally thousands of people climb the tower every year, and the authorities receive tons of mail asking bizarre questions. A look into the mailbag reveals a letter from a Turkish architect wanting to be told the mystical mathematical formulae used for the tower's structure. The Washington Monument was previously the tallest building in the world, but the Eiffel Tower was nearly twice the height. When Gustave Eiffel died in 1923, it was still the tallest tower and remained so for exactly 40 years. It was at last dethroned by the 1,046-foot Chrysler Building in New York, followed two years later by the Empire State Building.

☞ *Eiffel Tower, 75007, metro Champs-de-Mars (see map, p. 78), open 9:30am–11pm every day.*

THE TUILERIES GARDENS

As Dan Brown says, the name of the gardens refers to tiles that were manufactured here, made from the clay pits along the banks of the Seine. The area became a royal garden during the reign of Catherine de Medici. The gardens were redesigned in the 1660s by one of France's greatest gardeners, André Le Nôtre. Walk along the central alley. Practical tip: Do not take your car into the gardens unless your name is Collet or you work for the French FBI. At the Louvre end of the gardens is a beautiful collection of sculptures by Aristide Maillol. He is the master of the "pagan sacred feminine" who eulogizes the strength and beauty of women. Look for his fertility goddess *Pomona*, a nude figure holding an apple in each hand. At the age of 74 he met a 15-year-old beauty who became his new source of inspiration and who gave him a new lease on life. His muse, called Dina Vierny, inherited much of his work and has opened her art collection to the public. This is now the magnificent Maillol Museum.

☞ *Tuileries Gardens, 75001, metro Tuileries or Concorde.*
☞ *Maillol Museum, 61 rue de Grenelle, 75007, metro Rue-du-Bac (see map, p. 79), 11am–6pm, closed Tuesdays.*

THE CARROUSEL ARCH

Dan Brown mentions orgiastic rituals here. The arch is certainly not known for this in Paris, but it may just be a personal experience of Brown's! The Carrousel takes its name from a special equestrian display held to celebrate the birth of the Grand Dauphin, Louis XIV's son. The arch itself was built to commemorate the battle of Austerlitz and was used as a ceremonial entrance into the central courtyard of the Tuileries Palace. As Langdon is raced around the arch, he

reflects on four of the greatest art museums in Paris. He says they can be seen from here: Orsay, Louvre, and Jeu de Paume can be seen, but to see the Pompidou Centre, you need to walk a bit farther. The bronze statues on top of the arch are copies of the horses from St-Mark's basilica in Venice. Napoleon stole them thinking they would look better in Paris, but they have since been returned and replaced with copies. Stop a while beneath the arch and admire the truly spectacular vista from the pyramid of the Louvre to the Arc de Triomphe.

At this point you can enter the Louvre by taking the subterranean entrances on either side of the arch. (☞ *You can continue your tour by following the guided tour in the* Under the Pyramids *chapter.*) Before coming to the Louvre entrance, you arrive at the Carrousel underground shopping mall, where there is a large cafeteria and plenty of catering options in the main pyramid complex. The tourist office is by the inverted pyramid, and toilets can be found in this area.

☞ *If you prefer to stay aboveground, the pleasant café Le Nemours is under the arcades at the place Colette beside the Palais-Royal. Inexpensive lunches and good service are available; the café is next to the meridian marker of the rue St-Honoré.*

TOUR 2:
Langdon and Sophie Escape from the Louvre—The Itinerary

Begin your tour by attempting to jump from the toilet window in the Italian paintings gallery, between rooms 19 and 20 in the Denon wing. Before escaping, Sophie looks out of the window and marvels at the sight of the Eiffel Tower, the Sacré-Cœur, and the Arc de Triomphe, another mystical triangle in Paris. Admire the view before you jump, or if you prefer, take the exit that Sophie and Langdon really use. Follow signs to the Porte des Lions. This trail can be followed on foot and by city bus. Details of the sites and monuments are given in full after the itinerary.

Start at the pyramid and walk through the passageway of the Richelieu Wing to rue de Rivoli. Cross the street and walk westward beneath the lovely arcades to place de la Concorde. This takes about 20 minutes, or take a number 72 bus, three stops to Concorde. Stop at Concorde and walk to the central obelisk for the marvelous views. Cross the square northward to the corner of rue Royale and the square to get to the Hôtel Crillon. Continue along rue Gabriel, past the American Embassy, or take the number 52 bus from in front of the Hôtel Crillon, ride for two stops, get off, and walk back along avenue Matignon to the Champs-Élysées. Continue to the Arc de Triomphe on foot or take bus number 73 at the Matignon/Champs-Élysées intersection. Get off the bus at Étoile to visit the Arc de Triomphe.

RUE DE RIVOLI

The arcaded rue de Rivoli is named after a Napoleonic victory in Italy. It was once lined with splendid shops selling luxury goods, but it is now a jumble of perfumeries, clothes shops, and souvenir boutiques. The road is one of the few new ones built during the reign of Napoleon.

☞ *As Sophie and Langdon raced along the street, they had no time to stop, but on their return, they may have popped into elegant Angelina's tearoom for an old-fashioned hot chocolate or one of its famous Montblanc cakes, which have become an*

institution in Paris. Angelina's is at 226 rue de Rivoli, 75001, between metro Concorde and Tuileries.

PLACE DE LA CONCORDE: THE LARGEST SQUARE IN PARIS

Sophie and Langdon race around the square, having momentarily shaken off the police. In each corner of the square stands a colossal statue representing great towns in the different regions of France. The town of Strasbourg is a portrait of actress Juliette Drouet, long-term muse and mistress of Grand Master Victor Hugo.

HÔTEL CRILLON AND THE NAVAL MINISTRY

They pass the Hôtel Crillon, one of the finest and most expensive in Paris, at 10 place de la Concorde. The guest book here is a *Who's Who* of presidents and royalty. The Crillon is one of two identical buildings on either side of rue Royale; to the right is the Naval Ministry. This was once the furniture store of the royal family. The building was sacked during the Revolution in 1792, and at this time the crown jewels were stolen. The square was host to the public wedding celebrations of Louis XVI and Marie Antoinette, and it was also the location of the guillotine, first put here in 1792 to execute the thieves who had stolen the crown jewels. During the Revolution, 1,119 people were beheaded here in two years. The easternmost end of this building, bordering rue Royale, is the Hôtel de Coislin. Here on February 6, 1778, a small group of French and Americans gathered to sign a treaty that marked the success of Benjamin Franklin's attempts to enlist the help of France for achieving independence. The Treaty of Friendship, Commerce, and Alliance made France the first nation to recognize American independence. Strangely enough, the treaty was signed in the apartment of a man named Dean, whose Christian name was . . . Silas.

OBELISK OF LUXOR

The obelisk in the center of the square is about 3,000 years old. The carved hieroglyphics make references to Ramses II, enabling it to be dated. Hieroglyphs were decoded for the first time by the French Egyptologist Champollion. The obelisk was brought here from the Temple of Luxor in Egypt and erected in 1836. Transport of the obelisk and its erection (more phallic symbolism for Langdon to contemplate) were both incredible feats of engineering. The method of raising the obelisk is engraved in gold on the base of the plinth. The French astronomer Camille Flammarion planned to create a meridian here and turn the obelisk into the world's largest sundial. World War I put an end to the project.

AMERICAN EMBASSY

Sophie hopes to deliver Langdon to safety at the American Embassy, but seeing that the building is surrounded by police they turn back. The modern embassy, in one of the most prestigious locations in Paris, was built between 1931 and

1933. The building originally on this site was the private town house of Grimod de La Reynière. This man was a celebrated "gastronome" who became the first official restaurant critic in history. It is he who advised restaurants that if you gave a dish a fancy name you could charge twice the price. On May 22, 1927, Charles Lindbergh made a speech from the embassy balcony. Thousands of cheering Parisians had come to celebrate the first successful Atlantic crossing. (☞ *For more on Lindbergh see* Le Bourget *in the* Château Villette and Beyond *chapter.*)

CHAMPS-ÉLYSÉES

As Langdon is driven up the Champs-Élysées, he "sat white-knuckled in the passenger seat," as any right-minded person would, being driven in this part of town. The Champs-Élysées meant paradise to the ancients. It became a huge open-air theater during Napoleon's reign, the road forming the stage and the arch making the backdrop. It is famous for its shops and cafés and is equally beautiful at night, at which time it is referred to as "The Avenue of Rubies and Diamonds." Visit it at night to see why. The Champs-Élysées grew to extend the axis of Paris, which developed from the center of the Louvre. It

The Gallion, symbol of Paris (Carnavalet Museum)

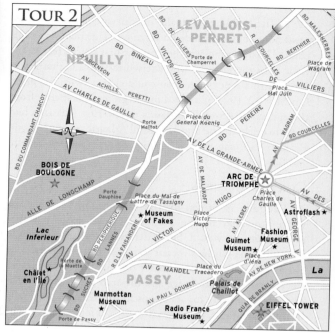

leads directly to another royal domain, St-Germain-en-Laye, so called because it forms an ancient and mysterious ley line.

The Arc de Triomphe: A Symbol of Paris

As Langdon and Sophie drive around the Arc de Triomphe, the time is exactly 2:51am; 2:50 is a well-known clock setting to watch sellers. If a watch is set at 10 minutes to 3, the hands form the shape of a smile, and the watch face looks friendly. This is a subliminal way to make the watch seem more attractive. But for Brown there is another meaning; not only does the shape make the form of the chalice he and Sophie are seeking, but as it is 2:51, the numbers add up to 8, the symbolic number of superperfection. The watch is a Disney timepiece featuring Mickey Mouse. Dan Brown mentions that Disney made much use of symbolism in films, drawing parallels between the Little Mermaid and Mary Magdalene. The initials of Mickey Mouse need no comment.

The arch was commissioned by Napoleon in 1806 as a symbol of the honor of the French Army. The architect

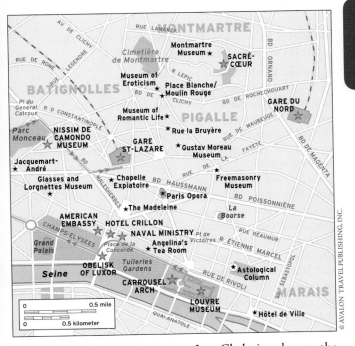

who won the commission was Jean Chalgrin, who was the man who finished St-Sulpice. A recent guidebook to Paris describes the monument as Napoleon's magical temple consecrated to the gods of war. Grand Master Victor Hugo's catafalque was placed under the Arc de Triomphe for one night, while a circle of 40 poets stood in vigil. As the funeral cortège wended its way to the Pantheon, two million people crowded the streets waving banners inscribed with the name of his works. The flame of remembrance on the tomb of the unknown soldier was first lit here on November 11, 1923. At exactly 7:30am on August 7, 1919, Charles Godefroy flew his Nieuport biplane, with a wingspan of 8.22 meters, through the 14-meter-wide opening. This was a symbolic act drawing attention to the plight of pilots at the end of the war. Several famous pilots had considered the stunt, including aviator Roland Garros, but balked at the attempt, believing it was too dangerous.

☞ *To visit the arch, take the underpass at the top right hand of the Champs-Élysées. Climb to the top—the view is superb.*

AVENUE WAGRAM, BOULEVARD COURCELLES, AND PARC MONCEAU

From the Etoile, Sophie and Langdon race down to gare St-Lazare. You can make the same journey by taking a number 30 bus. As you ride along the avenues and boulevards you will pass by magnificent Haussmannian façades, driving through one of the most elegant and expensive quarters of the city. This is also the diplomatic quarter where Sophie and Langdon career round the streets in their SmartCar before getting back to the Champs-Élysées. Rub shoulders with elegant society by taking the number 30 bus from the corner of Etoile and avenue Wagram, and alight at Monceau. The parc Monceau, where the first parachute landing in history took place, is one of the most delightful parks in Paris, and it is full of curiosities. It has some of the most unusual trees in Paris: a plane tree with a circumference of eight meters, an age-old gingko, and a spectacular handkerchief tree. The gateway into the park is an old security lookout post from the Louis XVI city wall; it also houses useful toilet facilities. There is a statue of best-selling author . . . no, not Dan Brown, but Guy de Maupassant. Also, look out for the romantic ruined colonnade, part of the ancient Tuileries Palace destroyed during the Commune, which makes an attractive frame for the lake. There is a fascinating philosopher's garden thought to be designed in the 18th century by the imaginative gardener Louis Carmontelle. This consists of iconography dear to Dan Brown: There are an obelisk, a pyramid, and a tomb, just like the one in Nicolas Poussin's painting *The Shepherds of Arcadia* and also at Rennes-le-Château. Could this be the tomb of Mary Magdalene?

The area surrounding the park is full of sumptuous private mansions, many of which have become museums, embassies, and consulates. One of the city's most delightful "off-the-beaten-track" museums is beside the park. The Nissim de Camondo Museum is a private collection of 18th-century furnishings and objects that would be a perfect evocation of life in Château Villette. You can also visit the lovely old-fashioned kitchens. The collections are laid out in a private town house left to the nation by a wealthy

Jewish banker, Moïse de Camondo, in memory of his son, who died in active service during World War I. His daughter and her family perished at Auschwitz.

☞ *Nissim de Camondo Museum, 63 rue de Monceau, 75008, metro Villiers or Monceau.*

To get to the next location get on the number 94 bus from the corner of parc Monceau and boulevard Malesherbes, and alight at gare St-Lazare.

GARE ST-LAZARE AND GARE DU NORD

At gare St-Lazare, Sophie and Langdon manage to throw off the police, buy train tickets to Lille, and then take a taxi from the side exit of the station. Trains for Lille leave from gare du Nord, and this is where Collet goes to wait for them. They are by now well on their way to the Zurich Bank.

As you enter the station via its grand façade, admire two modern art sculptures by Arman: a huge pillar of suitcases and a pillar of clocks *Time and Luggage—The Nightmare of Travel.* Once in the station, buy a ticket for Lille using your credit card (preferably your partner's), tear the ticket into shreds, and then leave the station by the exit marked rue de Rome. Get in the taxi whose driver you have previously bribed and ask him to take you to Montmartre. If you prefer, take the metro line 12 from St-Lazare to Pigalle. From Pigalle you can continue your tour by taking the Montmartrobus, which will give you a full tour of the village, taking about an hour for the round-trip. The bus goes by the picturesque vineyard, the Sacré-Cœur, and also stops at the Museum of Montmartre. The bus brings you back to Pigalle station.

SACRÉ-CŒUR AND MONTMARTRE

The huge Sacré-Cœur church dominates the hilltop of Montmartre. Langdon and Sophie speed past it as they head on their way to Saunière's bank. This Catholic church was built by popular subscription at the end of the Franco–Prussian War but not completed and consecrated until 1919. The biggest bell in the world, La Savoyarde, is housed in the minaret-style bell tower. The architect Paul Abadie was inspired by restoration work he had been doing in the south of France on a Byzantine-style basilica called St-Front de Perigeux. The great dome can be visited (83 meters high), and after a long climb the lookout turret offers some of the most spectacular but vertiginous views available anywhere in Paris.

Sacré-Cœur, 35 rue du Chevalier de la Barre, 75018.

This area is one of the most attractive in Paris and is well worth taking the time to visit. In the 19th and early 20th century this quarter was home to impressionists, postimpressionists, and modernists, including Pablo Picasso, Vincent Van Gogh, and Pierre-Auguste Renoir. Picasso painted his masterpiece *Les Demoiselles d'Avignon* in his studio at the Bateau Lavoir in Montmartre. In *The Da Vinci Code*, the anagram of this work is "Vile Meaningless

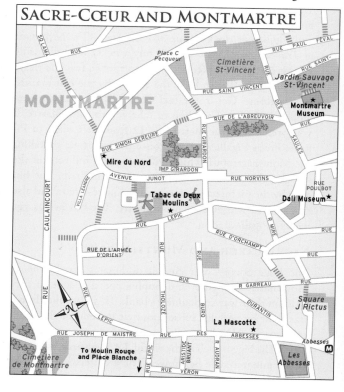

SACRE-CŒUR AND MONTMARTRE

Doodles." Paris Walks offers regular guided walks here on Wednesdays and Sundays if you would like to explore the village in more detail.

Montmartre is one of the "hundred villages" that make up Paris and it has very much its own personality and character. There is a natural outcrop of gypsum rock here, which was quarried till the 19th century. The quarries produced the famous plaster of Paris. The plaster works were at the bottom of the hill—the area was always snowy white—and the square is still called "place Blanche" today. There is a metro here, a convenient point at which to start a visit of the village, and it is also the location of the Moulin Rouge. The profession that Teabing says the church foisted on Mary Magdalene is also practiced here. The red-light district stretches from Blanche to Pigalle. At night, the brash neon lights flash, the stores have runners on the pavement to entice you behind the curtained store

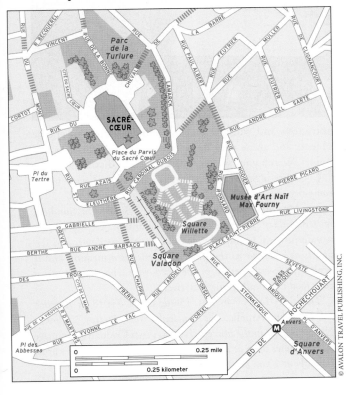

© AVALON TRAVEL PUBLISHING, INC.

entrances, and window displays show a variety of stange objects and some very impractical clothing (for over 18s only!). Watch your wallet in the red-light district.

☞ *For a Sunday lunch and a glass of good wine in the company of a colorful local crowd:*

La Mascotte, 52 rue des Abbesses, 75018. On Sundays, retired builder "Florence" plays the accordian, keeping alive a wonderful local tradition. Good lunches are available, and service is as eccentric as the clients! Florence is a medium and is probably the only person in the restaurant who can tell you if your food is actually going to arrive.

Tabac des Deux Moulins, 15 rue Lepic, 75018, is Amélie's café in the film Amélie. The principal actress, Audrey Tautou, is playing Sophie in the film of The Da Vinci Code. Montmartre always comes alive at aperitif time on Sundays, in other words, from about 10am onward!

OFF TO THE BOIS
DE BOULOGNE

Arriving at the Bois, Sophie and Langdon realize that the police are onto them, and they are obliged to hijack their driver's taxi. This is definitely the recommended way to get a cab in Paris, particularly at rush hour or on the many public transport strike days. The Bois is another of the beautiful parks of Paris. It is one of the "lungs" of the city, created by Adolphe Alphand during Baron Georges Haussmann's reurbanization project. Parisians come here for cycling, jogging, and dog walking. Chic Parisians take the little ferryboat to have tea at the Châlet en l'Île, on the island in the lake. As Dan Brown warns his readers, the park is best not visited at night, unless you know what you are letting yourself in for.

THE DEPOSITORY BANK OF ZURICH

It does have a website, but despite appearing conscientious about customer service, it seems very difficult to get through to anyone and impossible to open an account.

Sophie and Langdon's Guide to Occult Paris

Occult (see *Collins English Dictionary*): of or characteristic of magical, mystical, or supernatural arts, phenomena or influences.

The left and right banks of Paris have very different personalities. The right bank is much larger (14 of Paris's 20 arrondissements, as opposed to six on the left bank). Paris was founded on the Île de la Cité, where there is evidence of the Celtic Parisii's having settled. (☞ See the Cluny Museum of Medieval Art *under* Sophie and Langdon's Left Bank *in this chapter and the* Carnavalet Museum *in the* Isis and the Sacred Feminine *appendix.*) In Roman times, Paris spread to the left bank, the right bank being boggy marshes beneath the floodplain of the Seine River. The left bank, a hill of high and dry grounds, was more easily accessible as the Seine is narrower and shallower between la Cité and the south bank. This meant that bridges could more easily be built. The Petit Pont near Notre-Dame is the oldest crossing point in Paris.

The Roman city was divided into quarters by its two main streets, the *cardo* and *decumanus*. This is why the heart of the left bank is called the Latin Quarter today. A huge paving stone from the Roman road is embedded in the courtyard of the Church of St-Julian the Poor.

In the medieval period, development shifted to the right bank. This became an important economic center, boundaries of which continued to grow right up until the 19th century. By this period the flooding had subsided and the land had been reclaimed. The river, deep and wide between la Cité and the right bank, was easily navigable, and trading boats and ships could dock in this natural port. As goods were unloaded and traded on the river banks (*la grève*), this area became a huge and ever-expanding market. The man in charge of trading and taxation was named the chief merchant of Paris; his sumptuous mansion was built on the edge of the market square, which developed into the building now called Hôtel-de-Ville.

Both the squares in front of and behind this building were part of the market. When traders and marketeers were angry with conditions, they came here to *la grève* to manifest their displeasure; this is why the modern word for "strike" in French is *grève!* The money changers and bankers worked in the open air on the little square, place St-Gervais. Their symbol was the elm. It can be seen in the lovely ironwork balustrades along rue François-Miron, which runs beside the Church of St-Gervais–St-Protais, and an elm tree still grows in the middle of the square. In the 1180s the market was causing such congestion in the center that it was shifted farther north, just inside the medieval city walls.

The market consisted of huge roofed barnlike halls and is the "Les Halles" of Paris today. A huge feudal tower called the Tower of John the Fearless is evidence of the city's ancient rampart wall. The tower can be seen on the northern edge of the market today, and this wall formed the boundary of the right bank until the mid-14th century.

Paris kept growing and a ring of new walls was constructed around the right bank in the 1380s (including the Marais) and again in the 17th century along what is now "les grands boulevards." The 18th-century wall was Louis XVI's infamous ring of tollgates and the 19th-century wall can still be traced around the city just within the modern-day perimeter, which is the ring road now called the *périphérique*.

For a thumbnail history of Paris that is both beautiful and fascinating, visit the multimedia show *Paris Story* at 11 rue Scribe, 75009, metro Opéra (see map, p. 20); 10am–7pm, every hour on the hour, English commentary available. You will discover Paris in the company of one of its most illustrious Priory of Sion grand masters, Victor Hugo.

ÎLE DE LA CITÉ

The Île de la Cité is like a great ship afloat in the river. It is believed that the Gauls compared it to the boat used by Isis to seek her lost husband Osiris. (☞ *Her story is told in the Under the Pyramids chapter.*) The following circuit shows the Gallo–Roman rampart walls, Notre-Dame and its treasury,

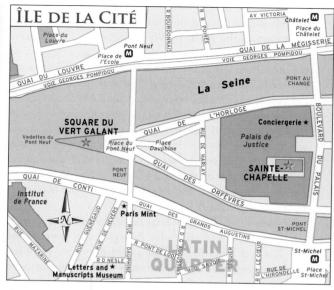

the Ste-Chapelle, Point Zero, and the site where the grand master of the Knights Templar was burned at the stake.

RUE DE LA COLOMBE

Traces of the city's most ancient rampart wall can be seen in the archaeological crypt museum beneath the parvis of Notre-Dame and on the charming rue de la Colombe. This wall was probably built toward the end of the 2nd or beginning of the 3rd century AD and was constructed from stone recovered by the Romans from their own monuments. The remains of the wall are spectacular. A close look reveals some of the building techniques used: Small holes and grooves were used for the insertion of lifting equipment and the fitting of huge metal staples to reinforce its structure. Some of the most decorative stone blocks come from the old forum of Roman Paris. The wall was built around the island to protect the city at the time of the barbarian invasions. The main temple of the Roman city, dedicated to Jupiter, was on the eastern end of the island where Notre-Dame stands today. Walk along the delightful rue de la Colombe to see a small mosaic of paving stones that crosses the street; this marks the location of the northern part of the wall.

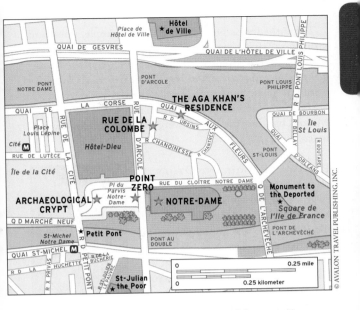

© AVALON TRAVEL PUBLISHING, INC.

NOTRE-DAME: THE TEMPLE OF VENUS, ISIS, AND THE GODDESS REASON

Notre-Dame, built between 1163 and the 1220s, is not without its own mysteries. The 20th century's most prominent alchemist, Fulcanelli, believed that the cathedral was a book in stone, "a hermetic masterpiece." He wrote that medieval alchemists used to meet in front of the right-hand portal, and that the sculptures there are an encyclopedia of hermetic knowledge.

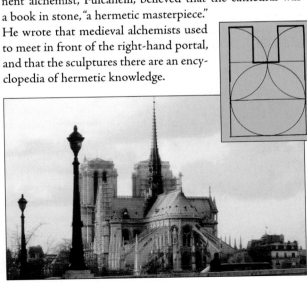

The cathedral is built according to a simple, pure, and visually satisfying geometric plan. The architectural complexities of the Golden Section were known to the ancients and rediscovered in the classical period, but they were unknown by the medieval cathedral builders. (☞ *See* Golden Numbers *in the* Beneath the Rose Line *chapter.*) Masons building the church were sworn to secrecy by their masters.

FESTIVAL OF FOOLS AND OTHER PAGAN SUBJECTS

A group of strange sculptures can be seen to the right of the central portal. They allude to the annual festival of fools that took place here. This was a social safety valve to keep different levels of society in their places. Everyone got the chance to break the rules of convention. Sex, violence, and drunkenness characterized the occasion; people cross-dressed, a pope of fools was elected, and nobility dressed as the poor and vice versa. This sculpted group shows a female devil urinating on the heads of a king, a bishop, and an ordinary man. The figures represent the three estates, or principal classes, and the message is that even kings and bishops can go to hell if they do not behave themselves.

ALCHEMISTS AND THEIR SYMBOLS

At the foot of the statue of Christ on the central pillar of the central portal is a strange allegory of alchemy. The figure in a circular medallion is holding two books, one open, one closed. Rising from his lap is a ladder. The closed book symbolizes esoterism, the open exoterism. The ladder represents the hieroglyph of patience, symbolizing the nine steps of patience the student of alchemy needs while working to achieve perfect knowledge.

WHICH HAND?

The left and right sides of the cathedral are associated with good and evil. In Latin, the word for "left" is *sinister* and associated with evil. Spilled salt is thrown over the left-hand shoulder so that it goes into the eye of the devil. On the central portal, all the virtuous can be seen on Christ's right-hand side, and the damned enter the gates of hell on his left. To visit the cathedral, you enter through the evil side, on Christ's left, and leave purified through the good portal, on Christ's right.

ISIS AND VENUS

Here Langdon and Teabing would be in their element! There is an astrological calendar in the rose window. It would be usual for it to begin with the sign of the ram, Aries, but here it begins with Pisces, which is apparently a Hindu tradition. Pisces is the astrological sign of mysticism and symbolizes the union of the self with the universal soul; it is also the symbol of Venus in Greek mythology. The lunar cycle of Venus and Isis also appears in the Gallery of Kings beneath the rose window. The gallery consists of 28 kings, whereas according to the Bible, there should be 18 or 19. The lunar month of Venus has 28 days. Pisces also appears carved on the left portal.

ALBIGENSIANS AND KNIGHTS TEMPLAR

On April 12, 1229, Raymond VII, the count of Toulouse, came here to swear before St-Louis and Blanche de Castille that he would respect a treaty he had signed that confirmed his defeat and his putting an end to the Albigensian Crusades. The Albigensians were Cathars, and as Brown tells us, believed that Christ and Mary Magdalene were married. The Albigensians were crushed during the early 13th-century crusades against them.

On March 18, 1314, Jacques de Molay, grand master of the Templars, and three other dignitaries were brought to the front of the cathedral before the king. The papal edict of the Templars' dissolution and confinement to perpetual imprisonment was read aloud. Molay began to proclaim his innocence, saying that his confession had been extracted under torture. The crowd began to riot, and Philippe le Bel (Philip IV) ordered him and 37 other Templars to be burned at the stake. (☞ *See* Square du Vert Galant: Kings and Templars.)

A PAGAN TEMPLE

During the French Revolution the cathedral became a pagan temple dedicated to the goddess Reason. A five-meter-high mountain was built in the nave, upon which a model antique-style temple was built. The temple symbolized philos-

The Synagogue

The Church

The Tree of Knowledge

The Funeral of the Virgin

ophy, and its priestess was a dancer from the Opera called Mademoiselle Aubry. She wore a white gown and a Phrygian cap. The cap, once worn by freed Roman slaves, had become an important symbol of liberty. The cathedral was returned to the Catholics in 1801.

☞ *Notre-Dame—The Towers, metro Cité, 9:30am–7:30pm every day.*
☞ *Notre-Dame Museum (history of the cathedral), 10 rue du Cloître-Notre-Dame, 75004, metro Cité, open 2:30–6pm Wednesdays, Saturdays, and Sundays.*
☞ *Archaeological Crypt Notre-Dame, 1 place du Parvis, 75004, metro Cité.*

POINT ZERO

A brass stud just in front of the façade of the cathedral marks the geographical center of Paris. It is the point from which distances to outlying towns are measured. The plaque has become worn away as it is traditional to stand upon it and make a wish. (Beware! Your wish will definitely come true; the author stood on this stone 15 years ago and has been married ever since.)

THE STE-CHAPELLE: KINGS, CHRIST, AND CONSTANTINE

The Ste-Chapelle is home to some of the best-preserved stained-glass windows to have survived from the medieval period. This spectacular building was constructed for the pious king Louis IX, who had just negotiated the purchase of a collection of some of the most precious holy relics in Christendom. In 1239, the Crown of Thorns, part of the holy spear, and a fragment of the true cross were brought to Paris by the king and his brother. The Ste-Chapelle was conceived as a giant reliquary case in which the relics could be kept and displayed. It is impossible to date the building exactly, but there is evidence that the construction had begun by 1246 and that the church was consecrated by 1248. It is estimated to have taken about six years to build. The chapel is built on two levels; the lower chapel was for staff and servants, and the upper was the private chapel of the king where the relics were kept. The ciborium, on which the relics were displayed, can still be seen. It is modeled on the building itself, having its own lower and upper levels, the latter being where the relics were placed. They are now kept in the treasury of Notre-Dame. There are 12 statues of the apostles, one on each of the main pillars, which symbolizes that the apostles are the pillars of the church.

The Windows

The windows date from two different periods. The tall lancets around the nave are mid-13th century and the west rose is 15th century. The lancets mostly tell stories from the Old Testament. This is curious, as the Old Testament on its own was seen as the book of the infidels. The stories are told from the bottom to the top of the window and read from left to right at each level. One window telling a story not taken from the Bible is read from the bottom to the top, but it zigzags from right to left and left to right. This is first on the right as you enter the upper chapel. It tells the story of the relics, from their acquisition by Constantine in the 3rd century to their arrival at the Ste-Chapelle in the 13th century. The rose window tells the story of the Apocalypse. (☞ *For more information see the discussion of symbols in the* Seven Seals *appendix.*) The predominant color in the glass is emerald green, which symbolizes the throne of God as described in Revelation 4:3, where John sees God in a rainbow of emerald light. The throne and its accompanying symbols can be seen in the center of the rose window.

Concerts are performed in the upper chapel and this is a beautiful and atmospheric way to experience the building.

☞ *Ste-Chapelle, 4 boulevard du Palais, 75001, metro Cité, open every day, with regular evening concerts.*

THE AGA KHAN'S RESIDENCE: HEADQUARTERS OF A MYSTERIOUS SECT

The house standing here has some of the most glorious views in Paris. It is best seen from the westernmost tip of the Île St-Louis. Although this building is made up from recovered medieval architectural elements, it was built by a French architect called Ferdinand Pouillon in 1956. The architect lived here for a year before it was purchased by the Aga Khan. This is the title of the hereditary head of the Ismailian sect of Muslims, who trace their origins to the tribe of the medieval Assassins. Ismailis are adherents of a secret Islamic sect, a branch of the Shiites also known as the Seveners, which retains its own secret traditions and rites. Prince Aly Khan married Rita Hayworth in the Mosque of Paris. The Mosque of Paris is well worth visiting. It is built around a courtyard and garden and has a splendidly exotic tearoom and garden. The minaret is 33 meters tall.

☞ *Aga Khan's Residence, 1–3 rue des Ursins, 75004, metro Cité.*
☞ *Mosque of Paris, place du Puits-de-l'Hermite, 75005, metro Jussieu (see map, p. 79), closed Tuesdays.*

SQUARE DU VERT GALANT: KINGS AND TEMPLARS

At the western end of the island, on the far side of Pont-Neuf, there is a small garden that offers spectacular views across the river and the west side of Paris. The square is named after Henry IV, whose nickname, Vert Galant, is an allusion to his youthful verve and lust for life. The statue of the king was made in the early 19th century from the bronze of the statue of Napoleon that had stood on top of the Vendôme Column. The artist who worked the metal for the new statue, Mesnel, is said to have hidden the words of antiroyalist songs in the horse's belly and a statue of Napoleon inside the king's right arm.

THE CURSE OF JACQUES DE MOLAY, GRAND MASTER OF THE TEMPLARS

Steps behind the statue lead down to the garden, where the last act of the story of the Templars was played out. On March 18, 1314, Philippe le Bel condemned Jacques de Molay to death. Molay and three of his companions were brutally burned at the stake here. The grand master called to the king, the pope, and his two ministers from his burning pyre. He demanded that they meet him before the court of God by the end of the year, and he went on to curse the kingdom and the dynasty. The terrible curse took effect. The pope died in agony on April 20, the king died after a curious hunting accident in November, Minister Nogaret died in mysterious circumstances a few days later, and Minister Marigny was

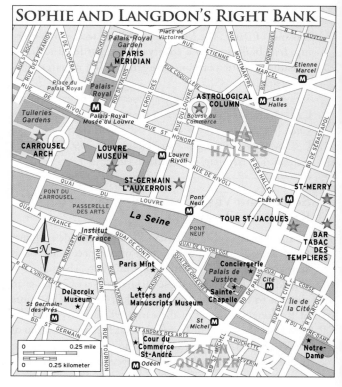

hung. Philippe le Bel's three sons died in quick succession, after short reigns, leaving only one male heir, who died after a couple of weeks. Charles IV, last son of Philippe le Bel, died in 1328 at the age of 33, bringing an end to the direct dynasty of Capetian kings and the start of a legendary tale of the power of the Knights Templar. (☞ *For a complete history of the Templars see* Square du Temple *under* Sophie and Langdon's Right Bank.)

SOPHIE AND LANGDON'S RIGHT BANK

BAR TABAC DES TEMPLIERS

The Bar Tabac des Templiers is a must for anyone with a taste for the unusual and a sense of curiosity about the mysterious knights. Teabing and Langdon would have felt at home here dicussing the Templars with the grand master of

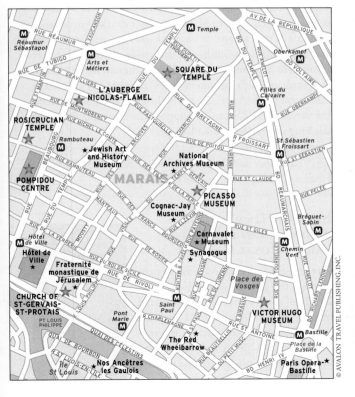

the café, Jacques Serre. This slightly scruffy café-museum has an incredible collection of jumbled objects, documents, and paintings that evoke royal history and that of the Templars. On either side of the doorway, as you enter, are copies of the last will and testament of Louis XVI; there are documents about the trial of Marie Antoinette; and Joan of Arc is an important symbol. The Templars evidently discovered the Turkish-style toilette on the Crusades and brought it back here with them. Here you can buy a T-shirt emblazoned with the Templars' crest, you can stand at the bar, sit down, or go to the counter to place your bets on the horse races. The café is guaranteed to be filled with an eccentric crowd and occasionally the author of this guide. If you wish to get involved in a discussion on the French monarchs, be warned that there are both legitimists and Orleanists in France. The café supports the legitimists, who hope to see a Bourbon on the throne. The Orleanists support the descendants of the last king of France, Louis Philippe.

Bar Tabac des Templiers, 35 rue de Rivoli, 75004, metro Hôtel-de-Ville, open 6am–2am every day.

BANG ON TIME!
A CANNON IN THE
PALAIS-ROYAL GARDEN

The original Paris Meridian runs through the gardens of Palais-Royal at 2° 20' 14" east of Greenwich and ahead of it by nine minutes and 21 seconds. A small cannon was fixed on the meridian line in 1786. A magnifying lens in line with the sun ignited the powder

and fired the cannon at exactly midday, enabling Parisians to set their watches. In recent years, the cannon was fired by hand as the lens had gone missing. Part of the mechanism was stolen in 1999 and all that remains today is its plinth and the barrel. (☞ *See* Meridian *under* Glossary *in the* Inside the Cryptex *appendix*.)

☞ *Palais-Royal, metro Palais-Royal-Musée-du-Louvre, in the garden area.*

CATHERINE DE MEDICI'S ASTROLOGICAL COLUMN AND A SELF-FULFILLING PROPHECY

The strange tower topped with a cagelike astrolabe is all that is left of a royal palace once known as l'Hôtel de la Reine, built for Catherine de Medici, who was a great believer in

astrology. The untimely death of her husband Henry II had been predicted by Pope Paul III's astrologer Luc Gauric, whose prediction was confirmed in a verse by Nostradamus. The queen appointed Nostradamus, doctor-astrologer, to her court in 1556. The two astrologers' predictions came true when Henry II died in a jousting accident in 1559. This reinforced her belief in the occult art. The strength of such beliefs is illustrated in the word "disaster." It comes from "Des Astres," meaning "from the stars," and shows how the position of the planets was thought to affect daily life. The court organized dances and parades in special formation according to star charts. When Nostradamus left the court she employed Cosimo Ruggieri as her astrological adviser and had this 31-meter tower built for him in the 1570s. Ruggieri in turn would foretell the death of the queen. He informed her that she would die near St-Germain. In Paris, the church of the Louvre was St-Germain l'Auxerrois, and her country residence was St-Germain-en-Laye, so she retreated to her château at Blois. Frail and worried after the long journey, she took to her bed and called the new abbot at the château to hear her confession. When she asked him his name he replied, "Julien de St-Germain." She promptly dropped dead!

🖙 *The Tower, Bourse du commerce, rue de Viarmes, 75001, metro Louvre-Rivoli.*

🖙 *If you wish to know what lies in store for you or a friend, go to Astroflash, 84 avenue des Champs-Élysées, metro Franklin D. Roosevelt (see map, p. 34). For a very reasonable price, you can buy an attractive and surprisingly revealing astrological chart, complete with analysis. Open seven days a week.*

THE CHAPELLE EXPIATOIRE

The chapel is a tranquil harbor of peace tucked away behind the noise and bustle of the St-Lazare station and the department store quarter. It was built for Louis XVI's brother, Louis XVIII, in memory of the martyred king and queen, and as its name suggests, it is a public request for forgiveness after the atrocities committed during the Revolution. It is here that Louis XVI and Marie Antoinette were buried after being executed, but much mystery surrounds what happened to them after their deaths, just as it surrounds Dan Brown's question of the Merovingians.

Originally the site had been the cemetery of the Madeleine Church, but its proximity to the guillotine meant that it soon became the communal grave for more than 1,000 people executed at the time. Among those whose bodies were unceremoniously thrown here were Madame Roland, Philippe Égalité, Camille Desmoulins, Georges-Jacques Danton, and Charlotte Corday, who assassinated Jean-Paul Marat.

Louis XVIII supposedly had the remains of his brother and sister-in-law disinterred and transported to the royal burial ground of St-Denis in 1815, 23 years after their execution. The number of those buried here and the passage of time would have made the bodies of the king and queen impossible to identify accurately. The other remains from the site were transported to the catacombs before the chapel was built in 1816, and it is very probable that their true remains lie there along with those of six million other Parisians.

More than 100 people were killed in a terrible accident during the wedding celebration of Marie Antoinette and Louis XVI, which was held on the Concorde Square. These unfortunates were buried here in the cemetery and it is strangely ironic that those victims should have remained side by side with the king and queen for more than 20 years. One thing is certain: This association of the monarchs with the Madeleine adds another string to Dan Brown's bow.

☞ *Chapelle Expiatoire, 29 rue Pasquier, 75008, metro St-Augustin (see map, p. 20).*
☞ *The Catacombs, metro Denfert-Rochereau (see map, p. 4), closed Mondays (skeleton staff only), dogs not allowed.*

THE LOCATIONS OF THE GUILLOTINE, THE PATRIOTIC SHORTENER

The guillotine was moved many times during the revolutionary years, as it needed solid foundations and level ground to function correctly. Five paving stones can be seen in the street by 16 rue Croix-Faubin. The first guillotine was set up in front of the Hôtel-de-Ville. For a while, it was where the Carrousel Arch is now, then at the Bastille and the place de la Nation.
☞ *A real military guillotine can be seen in the café La Guillotine at the Caveau des Oubliettes, on rue Galande (see map, p. 79). There are guillotine blades in the Police Museum (see map, p. 79) and the Conciergerie (see map, p. 45).*

HOUSE OF NICOLAS FLAMEL, GRAND MASTER OF THE PRIORY OF SION 1398–1418

Nicolas Flamel was Paris's most celebrated alchemist. One of his many properties, said to be the oldest house in Paris, is now a restaurant. Flamel was born in Pontoise, outside Paris, in 1330. He was an educated man who bought and sold manuscripts and seems to have worked as a public scribe. He generated immense riches, and sudden wealth at this period was often ascribed to alchemy. In fact, the goal of the alchemist (turning base metals into gold) was not financial but spiritual. The hermetic and mysterious world of al-  chemy was one of symbolism and allegory. The transmutation of materials symbolized a spiritual passage between man's terrestrial existence and a spiritual one.

The quest of the alchemist was also related to a search for immortality. An immortality pill was initially sought using refined mercury sulphide. This resulted in many deaths! Alchemists encouraged the development of accurate scientific equipment such as scales, clocks, measures, and temperature control, which were needed for their experiments. They thus contributed greatly to the world of medicine, chemistry, and pharmacology. They improved knowledge of dyeing, they probably invented fireworks and gunpowder, and they discovered anesthesia and distillation. The English philosopher and alchemist Roger Bacon is mentioned by Langdon to Sophie when they are trying to decrypt the messages left in the Louvre.

Flamel's career as an alchemist began after a dream in which an angel brought him a book illustrated with strange designs and told him, "You understand nothing in this work; no one else does, but one day you will see in it what no one else can." Shortly after this, a stranger came into his shop and offered him a manuscript to buy. Immediately he recognized this as the one in his dream. It turned out to be an alchemist's almanac. Suddenly filled with desire to pursue this dream, he built a laboratory and began to experiment. He recorded success at transmutation and then made a pilgrimage to Spain and met Jewish hermetic scholars. His great wealth, although mysterious, is evident because he became a generous benefactor, building porches onto churches, restoring the Cemetery of the Innocents in Paris, helping charitable foundations, and opening an alms house, which is now a restaurant on rue de Montmerency. His tombstone can be seen in the Cluny Museum. It was discovered at Les Halles when the market was demolished. It had been turned upside down and used as a chopping-board for shredding spinach. Flamel lived very near the tour St-Jacques, and the roads Flamel and Pernelle are named after him and his wife.

(Alchemists seek the philosopher's stone, the secret of eternal life. Nicolas Flamel and the philosopher's stone are central to one of the *Harry Potter* stories, and recently critics have referred to *The Da Vinci Code* as the *Harry Potter* for grown-ups.)

☞ *L'Auberge Nicolas-Flamel, 51 rue de Montmorency, 75003, metro Rambuteau or Arts et Metiers, closed Saturday afternoons and Sundays.*

THE MIRE DU NORD

The mire du nord is the northern marker of the old Paris meridian. It is a masonry pyramid three meters tall. It was installed on the top of the hill of Montmartre by Cassini, the first astronomer to realize that there were spaces between the rings of Saturn. It is difficult to get to as it is in a private residence, although the guardian is supposed to let visitors in on request. (Beware, the concierge who guards the access to the mire is aggressive; take a clove of garlic in case!)

☞ *The residence is at 1 avenue Junot (see map, p. 38) in the garden of the old windmill where Pierre-Auguste Renoir painted his famous work the* **Moulin de la Galette,** *now in the Musée d'Orsay.*

THE PICASSO MUSEUM

Jacques Saunière, though curator of the Louvre, was astonishingly no fan of modern art. He expresses his distaste for cubism through the brilliant anagram of Pablo Picasso's *Les Demoiselles d'Avignon,* which becomes "Vile Meaningless Doodles." Picasso would have been amused as the surrealists and Dadaists all loved wordplay and this was evident in their art. One of Picasso's closest friends was Jean Cocteau, grand master of the Priory of Sion. Cocteau took the idea of being a member of an elite group very seriously, whereas Picasso did not. Picasso proposed a design for Cocteau's sword when he was elected a member of the French Academy. It was in the form of a toilet seat.

Picasso was the first to glue and stick real objects onto his paintings, including words and phrases cut from newspapers and magazines. This made him the inventor of another new art form dear to modern artists: collage. His first work in this style, called *Chaise canée*, is at the Picasso Museum. The museum has a fantastic collection of the artist's work covering the whole of his life, from his childhood right up to his final period. Picasso died in 1973 at age 92 and had worked prolifically all his life. The museum has bought no works but is made up of a large part of the artist's private collection, bequeathed according to a French law called a *dation*. This means his heirs gave the works in lieu of death duties. Picasso never lived here and had no association with the building, but he owned several historic houses and châteaux and would undoubtedly have approved. The museum is laid out chronologically, enabling the visitor to follow each of the artist's brilliant periods. Key works of the museum include: two self-portraits, *La Fillette aux pieds Nus*, painted in 1895 when the artist was just 14 years old, *The Death of Casagemus*, a portrait of a friend who died shortly after Picasso's arrival in Paris. There is an entire room devoted to the development of cubism. There is also an elegant realist portrait of his wife, Olga, which shows he could do it when he tried! Sculptures and later works are displayed in the basement of the building, a beautiful 17th-century mansion. The building is known as the Hôtel Salé or Salty House, because its original owner made his fortune from administering the salt tax for Louis XIV.

Picasso Museum, Hôtel Salé, 5 rue de Thorigny, 75003, metro St-Paul, open 9:30am–6pm, closed Tuesdays.

THE POMPIDOU CENTRE

Langdon, perhaps keen on modern art, mentions the Pompidou Centre several times. As a symbologist, he would be keen to see the works of the symbolists, the surrealists, and Dadaists for whom the world of symbols was extremely important. He would have also studied Paul Klee and Wassily Kandinsky, who invented their own symbolic pictorial languages, and be able to discourse lengthily on the suprematist Kazimir Malevitch, who painted a white square on a white background.

The museum also has a collection of works by Yves Klein, who painted the first monochromes in his famous fluorescent blue. There are a few beautiful Jackson Pollock dripping paintings, too. Langdon would probably spend time contemplating the dark and strangely moving religious paintings of Georges Rouault.

The Pompidou Centre is itself a coded building. The architects, Richard Rogers and Renzo Piano, used the color codes of architectural plans to illustrate the purpose of each part of the building. Red indicates the moving parts such as escalators and lifts, green all the parts that carry water, yellow for all the electrics, and blue for air ducts and conditioning.

The building takes its inspiration from Notre-Dame and nearby St-Merry. Like these Gothic churches, all the structural elements are on the exterior of the building, leaving a vast open space inside for the museum displays.

The modern art museum was one of President Georges Pompidou's projects. He was very interested in modern art. A competition was held to find the best design. Of the 681 architects who entered the contest, only 20 were French.

Pompidou commissioned some ultramodern interior décor for the Elysée Palace, causing outrage among the traditionalists. A magnificent room designed for him by Yaacov Agam is now re-created here at the museum; see the salle Agam on the fourth floor.

The museum is divided into two levels. The fourth floor

shows art from the 1960s to the present day and the fifth floor displays work from the beginning of modern art (Henri Matisse and Picasso) to the 1960s. Spectacular views are available from the rooftop terrace.

☞ *Pompidou Centre, 75004, metro Hôtel-de-Ville, open 11am–9pm, closed Tuesdays.*

A ROSICRUCIAN TEMPLE

The Rosicrucians are another of the many religious sects that are mentioned frequently by Dan Brown. This esoteric movement spread across Europe in the early 17th century.

Two pamphlets printed in Germany around 1615 are attributed to a Christian Rosenkreutz (1378–1484). He claimed to possess occult powers based on scientific and alchemistic knowledge. He founded the order of the Rosy Cross and the pamphlet was used to recruit learned men.

The Rosicrucian Fraternity has existed in America since at least 1774. According to their own historical publications, they were led by a Great Council of Three. These included Benjamin Franklin, Thomas Paine, and later La Fayette.

Benjamin Franklin was a member of the Paris Rosicrucian Lodge "Humanidad." Thomas Paine lived at 10 rue de l'Odeon while he was in Paris. A plaque there reads: "Thomas Paine, English by birth, French by decree and American by adoption."

The Rosicrucians bring together, into one organization, the various associations of individuals known as Hermetists, Gnostics, Pythagoreans, magi, Platonists, and alchemists. They study philosophy and offer classes in astrology, the objective being to reconcile the mystical, the scientific, and the spiritual. They use a host of symbols, including the blade and chalice triangles.

☞ *The Rosicrucians' Paris bookshop and temple are at 199 rue St-Martin, around the corner from Nicolas Flamel's house and the Pompidou Centre. (It sells books, cards, incense, tarot cards, pendulums, crystals, music, etc.)*

ST-GERMAIN L'AUXERROIS

There was originally a Merovingian church on this site dedicated to St-Germain, bishop of Auxerre in the late 5th century.

The present Gothic church is an almanac of *Da Vinci Code*–style sculptures, carvings, and religious iconography. Outside the church on the north side is an extremely rare Ball of Rats (*Boule aux rats*). Only three are known in France. The sculpture shows rats gnawing away at a ball that may symbolize the bread of life or the world in general. The rats are being surveyed by a cat in hunting position.

The church is also home to a wonderful medieval bestiary of creatures. Look out for dancing bears, fantastical birds, griffins, monkeys, wolves, and dogs. At the rear end of the church, at the base of the roof, is a frieze with a sliced fish. This curious work alludes to the name of local benefactors, the Troncon family, whose name means "slice" in French.

In the porch is a statue of St-Mary the Egyptian. Her story is told in Jacques de Voragine's book *The Golden Legend*. This work, a medieval encyclopedia of the lives of the saints, is alluded to by Teabing.

The curious and beautiful statue shows Mary holding a stack of loaves. She was a prostitute who sold herself to earn money to go on a pilgrimage to the Holy Lands. On her arrival at the temple, she was pushed away by an invisible hand and told to go over the River Jordan into the desert. She stayed in the desert as a hermit and although

she could not read, she was divinely instructed in the Christian faith. She lived for many years on the bread she had taken with her. Her clothes had long been in tatters but her hair grew and covered her nudity. After several decades in the desert, she met a monk called Zosimus, who gave her his cloak and promised to return to give her communion. When he returned, he found her dead, but a friendly lion appeared and helped Zosimus dig her a grave. This story is painted by Théodore Chassériau in the lovely church of St-Merry.

Once the royal family moved to the Louvre, this church became the parish church of the palace. The royal pew can be seen inside the church in the northern-side aisle. Artists employed by the king at the Louvre were traditionally buried here; about 20 of France's most famous painters, sculptors, and architects were laid to rest here, among them Boucher and Chardin.

☞ *St-Germain l'Auxerrois, 75001, metro Louvre-Rivoli.*

St-Merry

Langdon and Teabing would have had great interest in this beautiful and mysterious church that is associated with two female saints whose stories may have come from that of Mary Magdalene. There is also an extraordinary head of Baphomet crowning the central portal of the façade, which itself is a riot of creatures: beetles, frogs, snails, and lizards that crawl up the doorway. Teabing mentions the symbolism of medieval church portals, saying they were seen as equivalents to a certain part of the female anatomy. (When Inspector Collet reads Teabing's notes, he remarks that it makes him feel like going back to church again.) Baphomet is one of the mysterious symbols associated with the Knights Templar. (☞ *His symbolism is explained in the* Glossary; *see the* Inside the Cryptex *appendix.*)

This church has the oldest bell in Paris (1331), called "the merry," which is in a small octogonal tower by the façade. The church has a beautiful organ and French composer Camille Saint-Saëns, who wrote the famous *Danse macabre*, was organist here for a while. Along the outside of the church on rue Cloître-St-Merry are fascinating gargoyles.

The corner of the church was notorious for its filth, squalor, and prostitutes in medieval times. In *Les Misérables*, Victor Hugo has his young hero Gavroche die on the corner that this street makes with the church. Inside the church is a 16th-century stained-glass window telling the story of St-Agnes, patron saint of prostitutes. (Look for the first windows in the upper row of the nave.) Agnes was forced into prostitution by the Roman emperor to punish her for her Christianity. Later, when his son was ill, the emperor called upon her to pray for the boy. This she did and he was cured. She can be seen in the window, shown like Mary the Egyptian, naked but clothed by her long hair. On the walls of the third chapel of the left-hand-side aisle are frescoes telling the story of Mary the Egyptian. (☞ *Her story is told in detail under* St-Germain l'Auxerrois.)

☞ *St-Merry, 75004, metro Hôtel-de-Ville.*

Square du Temple and the History of the Templars

The square du Temple is a key site in Paris. It was here that the headquarters of the Paris Templars was located. The ancient and spectacular temple buildings survived until after the Revolution, but tragically they were destroyed, probably because of their association with the royal family. Both Louis XVI and his son Louis XVII were imprisoned here. Marie Antoinette was kept here until the execution of the king. A poignant recreation of their prison cell can be seen at the Carnavalet Museum. Today all that remains of the Temple of Paris is a pleasant square, a covered market, and a few medieval streets. The Templars' compound was literally a city within the city.

The limits of the enclosure followed the streets around the present square: rue du Temple, rue de Picardie, rue de Bretagne, and rue Bérenger. The massive fortress and keep were at the crossroads of the rue Eugène Spuller and the rue Perrée at the southeastern corner of the lovely garden (square du Temple).

The castle was built in the 1260s, which is later than both the Louvre and Notre-Dame. Its size and stature reflected the political strength and the financial assets of the order. The Conciergerie on Île de la Cité gives an idea of what the temple building looked like. Its magnificent Gothic chamber, called the salle des Gendarmes, and the huge feudal towers on its façade were built for Philippe le Bel.

THE KNIGHTS TEMPLAR—GUARDIANS OF THE GRAIL

The origin of the Templars goes back to 1118, when nine French knights decided to devote their lives to protecting pilgrims on their perilous journey to the Holy Lands. Pilgrims had been traveling there since the Christianization of Europe. The city of Jerusalem, where Christ died and was resurrected, was the most important. A shrine had been built by Constantine around Christ's tomb; this and Golgotha attracted many pilgrims and accounts of their journeys exist from as early as the 4th century. Pilgrims carried staffs and wore cloaks with badges from the shrines they had visited. A collection of these badges can be seen in the Cluny Museum; many of them were found when the Seine was dredged. In 396 St-Jerome, who translated the Bible into Latin, built two monasteries to accommodate the ever-growing crowds.

In the 7th century the Muslim empire grew to include Palestine, Syria, and Egypt. Calife Omar took Jerusalem in 637, and during this expansion many churches were destroyed and Jerusalem became an important Muslim center. The Holy Sepulchre was spared because the Koran recognizes the sacred character of the teachings of Jesus. Pilgrimages continued through the reign of Charlemagne even though these were troubled times.

The situation for pilgrims changed dramatically when the Fatimids took Jerusalem in 969. The Calife al-Hâkîm, known for his brutality, destroyed the Holy Sepulchre and persecuted both Jews and Christians. As news of the situation filtered back to the Christian West there was outrage. The Byzantine Empire, occupied with its own wars with the Muslim Turks, was unable to intervene in the Holy Lands. Christian Europe was obliged to take action.

THE FIRST CRUSADES

Pilgrimages had by now become impossible, and massacres were frequent. In 1095, Pope Urban II called upon Christians to conquer the holy city once again. Neither king nor emperor replied, but feudal lords and dukes rallied to the call and prepared to depart. "God wills it," shouted the crowds. In August 1096, the journey began. It took three years for 12,000 men to arrive. Jerusalem was recaptured on July 15, 1099. These men wore red crosses cut from cloth that were sewn onto their tunics. The name crusade comes from the French word *croix*, meaning "cross."

One of the leaders of these men, Godefroy de Bouillon, was elected head of the "kingdom of Jerusalem." According to some sources, he is also the founder of the Priory of Sion and a Merovingian descendant of Christ and Mary Magdalene. He ordered the Knights Templar to retrieve the sangreal documents from beneath the temple to provide the Merovingians with proof that they did indeed have a hereditary link with Jesus. Godefroy de Bouillon died shortly after the taking of the city and was succeeded by his brother Baudoin. Pilgrims once again came, now traveling by ship, but on land there were still dangers. This is why in 1118 Hugues de Payns formed an order of knights to protect Christian pilgrims. They named themselves the Poor Knights of Christ. Their fame spread and soon Baudoin II (cousin of Baudoin I) offered them room in his palace where Solomon's Temple once stood. Not long after this he left them the whole palace and they renamed themselves the Knights of the Temple. At last they had full access to the treasure they were seeking.

The knights saw themselves as both warriors and monks. In 1127, Hugues de Payns requested official recognition from the pope. The order had increased in numbers and organization became a necessity. The warrior monks would adopt a rule championed by St-Bernard and a hierarchical structure based on their social rank when they joined. A uniform was adopted, consisting of a white tunic, with black or brown cloak, and the distinctive vermilion cross. In 1139, Pope Innocent II authorized the Templars to build their own oratories and have their own cemeteries. The chapels they built were simple, as was dictated by their adopted rule. The Templar churches were often round, as was the case in Paris and is still the case in London. They were based on the architecture of Christ's Holy Sepulchre. As the order grew, so did its wealth and independence. The Templars played the role of bankers, and in Paris the Templars looked after the treasury of the king. Their political and religious independence would eventually lead to a decline in their popularity and disastrously, to their being distrusted by king and pope.

Other nations formed their own groups, which led to conflict, and the Hospitallers and the Teutonic knights warred with the Templars. In 1229, Frederic II Hohenstaufen usurped the throne of Jerusalem, having himself crowned at the Holy Sepulchre. He was supported by the Teutonic knights but was excommunicated by the pope, and therefore hostilities ensued.

In 1244, Jerusalem was again attacked by the Turks. Jerusalem was lost again, and 312 Templars out of 348 lost their lives. Hope grew as the seventh crusade began, but this turned out to be a disaster, added to by the Nile flood, which caused a terrible epidemic of dysentery. The army perished, King St-Louis was taken prisoner, and the grand master of the temple died.

In 1288, the Mamalouks launched an offensive against the Holy Lands, and the Sultan al-Ashraf took St-Jean d'Acre in the spring of 1291 with an army of 220,000 men. Despite a reconciliation that united their force, the Hospitallers and the Templars fell. Guillaume de Beaujeu, the last Templar grand master to serve in the Holy Lands, was killed, as was the master of the Hospitallers. The surviving Templars left the Holy Lands for the last time.

THE TREASURE OF THE TEMPLARS

From the end of the 12th century to the end of the 13th century, the Temple of Paris held the treasury of the king and acted as bankers. The Knights' own wealth, added to that of donations and gifts, made them an immensely wealthy and powerful organization. Payments made to them by pilgrims for "safe conduct" was another considerable source of revenue.

But what was the treasure really? Some argue that it was the Holy Grail. The Grail consists of documents, including the famous Q document said to be written in Christ's own hand, diaries of Mary Magdalene, and proof that Mary Magdalene and Christ engendered a bloodline of (sangreal) descendants.

Part of the Grail is said to be the sarcophagus containing Mary Magdalene's relics. It may also have included the Ark of the Covenant. All these were purportedly found by the Templars when they had the temple in Jerusalem as their headquarters. The tomb in the Nicolas Poussin painting *Et in Arcadia Ego* and an actual tomb just like it at Rennes-le-Château suggested to the authors of *Holy Blood, Holy Grail* that the treasure may have been hidden at Rennes-le-Château and found by Bérenger Saunière.

PHILIPPE LE BEL (1285–1314) AND THE FALL OF THE TEMPLARS—FRIDAY THE 13TH

As a result of war and a desire to extend his boundaries, Philip IV, known as Philippe le Bel (Philip the Fair) was always desperately in need of money. He had obliged his financiers (the Templars) to collect taxes for him, which had in part contributed to their decline in popularity. Philippe fell into conflict with Pope Boniface VIII over clerical taxes and was excommunicated in 1303.

After the death of the next pope, Pope Benedict XI, a Frenchman, Clément V from Bordeaux, became pope and settled at Avignon. Owing his election to the king, the pope agreed upon the dissolution of the Templars. Philippe had already persecuted the Jews and Lombardy bankers to obtain their fortunes, and he now determined to acquire the great wealth of the Templars. Philippe argued that as they had lost the Holy Lands, their wealth no longer served any purpose. In a hugely successful secret operation, all French Templars were arrested at dawn on Friday, October 13, 1307. Since this event, a superstitious belief has been attached to Friday the 13th.

Tremendous coordination was essential, and the arrests were planned long in advance. Some argue that this

3. LA CONCIERGERIE — Salle des Gardes
Construite dans le style gothique. C'est par le perron qui se trouve à gauche que descendent les détenus à leur arrivée

was not done only for financial gain, but to suppress the controversial knowledge that the Templars held. As each grand master was arrested, the king installed one of his own administrators in each headquarters. In Paris, the chancellor Nogaret personally arrested Jacques de Molay. Templars from about 3,000 different locations were arrested on the same day, and at the same time, in a brilliantly orchestrated seizure.

The arrest of the Templars in 1307 did not bring an end to the story. There were trials, tortures, and confessions. Parisians were informed of the evil deeds perpetrated by the Templars. They were accused of blasphemy, obscene rites, and worshiping an idol named Baphomet. Spitting on the cross and sodomy were also among the crimes supposedly committed. In the lower chamber of the Parisian Templars' headquarters, 138 Paris Templars were interrogated; 36 prisoners died under torture and out of 138, only three denied the crimes of which they were accused. The evidence was conclusive: The Templars were guilty.

Several years of prevarication between king and pope would pass by while they squabbled over what would happen to the Templars' treasure. On December 22, 1312, Clement V delegated his power to three cardinals, all of whom were close to Philippe le Bel. The fate of the Templars was sealed, but then again, so was the king's.

The last act of this incredible tale is told at the site where it takes place. (☞ *See* Square du Vert Galant: Kings and Templars *under* Sophie and Langdon's Guide to Occult Paris.)

THE CHURCH OF ST-GERVAIS–ST-PROTAIS: THE ELM

St-Gervais–St-Protais is a lovely church situated just behind the Hôtel-de-Ville. The two saints were Christian twins martyred by the Roman Emperor Nero. An elm tree grows in the middle of the square in front of the church, which was traditionally the emblem of bankers, but it is also associated with the mystery of the Holy Grail.

The Priory of Sion is said to have disowned its protegés, the Templars, after the loss of Jerusalem in 1187. The Templars from this time onward were no longer the military arm of the Priory and no longer under its control. Which of the two parties held the treasure at this time is not known, but the Priory seems to have moved its headquarters to the medieval citadel of Gisors. At Gisors, a bizarre ceremony took place in 1188, which included the cutting down of a sacred elm tree said to be 800 years old. The felling of the tree is supposed to have symbolized the cutting of relations between the two groups. Until this time, the Priory and Templars had the same grand master, but from this date onward the connection ends. According to Priory documents, the first grand master was Jean de Gisors and this newly formed Priory also went by the name of Ormus. *Orme* means "elm" in French and Ormus is also an important symbol for Gnostics and Zoroastrians. According to the Masons, Ormus is an ancient Alexandrian mystic.

There are elm trees in the ironwork of the building here and elms are also carved into the misericords (choir stall seats) inside.

SHROUDED IN MYSTERY

The Turin Shroud has given rise to many of the theories developed in *The Da Vinci Code*. There is a full-size reproduction of the shroud in the Church of St-Gervais–St-Protais. One theory says that the shroud was made by Leonardo da Vinci and is in fact a self-portrait.

The inexplicable crease line across the neck was supposedly put there to reinforce da Vinci's unorthodox religious approach. The line alludes to the severed head of John the

Baptist, a figure to whom in his paintings he gives more importance than Christ.

Another theory is that the shroud was created when Jacques de Molay's body was wrapped after his crucifixion. The story is that Jacques de Molay was in fact not burned at the stake, but mocked and crucified like Christ, and then wrapped in a shroud that fused the chemicals found in human blood and in incense to form the image of the man's body. As eccentric and questionable as these theories are, there is still no satisfactory explanation as to exactly how the shroud may have come about. The church bookshop, on the rue des Barres, has several documents about the shroud. They are all as evasive as the next one when it comes to giving concrete information about this strange and ghostly object.

Church of St-Gervais–St-Protais, place St-Gervais, 75004, metro Hôtel-de-Ville.

THE TOUR ST-JACQUES

The tour St-Jacques was once part of the church of the local corporation of butchers at the nearby market. St-Jacques-de-la-Boucherie church was demolished at the end of the Revolution and the 50-meter-high tower is all that remains. St-Jacques was the patron of one of the most important pilgrimage shrines in medieval Europe, and the tower was the assembly point for pilgrims as they prepared to depart for St-Jacques de Compostella. The symbol of the pilgrims going to Compostella was the cockle shell, in French the *coquille St-Jacques!*

The tower is supposed to hold secrets for alchemists. Nicolas Flamel built a porch with strange figures carved on it. He was also buried at the church and his tombstone can be seen in the Cluny Museum. The tower attracts mediums and mystics of all kinds; perhaps they are the only ones who can penetrate the mystery of the building, which is forever under scaffolding.

The tower has had a checkered history. Blaise Pascal carried out his barometric experiments here in 1648. He was a Jansenist, and like Silas in *The Da Vinci Code*, practiced

self-mortification, dying after sufferings aggravated by this regimen. There is a statue of him at the base of the tower. He also invented history's first-ever calculator, which can be seen at the Musée des Arts and Metiers.

When revolutionaries wanted to recover the bronze of the bells, they burned the timbers so that the bells would fall, which they did, right through four floors of the Gothic vaulting! The tower has been hollow ever since. It was then used as a bullet factory. A foundry was set up at the top and lead was dropped in small quantities into vats of water below so that the droplets would cool. In 1836, this architectural curio was bought by the city of Paris and proclaimed a historic monument. The architect Ballu began restoring it in the 1850s and the work continues!

The medieval tetramorph that once crowned the tour St-Jacques is now in the gardens of the Cluny Museum. The tower is now a meteorological station attached to the observatory of Montsouris.

Tour St-Jacques, square de la Tour St-Jacques, 75004, metro Châtelet.

VICTOR HUGO (GRAND MASTER OF THE PRIORY OF SION 1844–1885)

Hugo occupied an apartment on the second floor of a lovely pavilion on the place des Vosges. This is now a museum and entrance is free. A long suite of rooms, one after the other, runs from an antechamber, through living rooms, to his bedroom. This room contains the bed in which he died. The rooms are dark and the atmosphere is oppressive and spooky. This is heightened by massive pieces of fantastic and

place des Vosges

imaginative furniture dreamed up by Hugo in an antique style. A mysterious and magnificent paneled room was made by Hugo for his mistress, Juliette Drouet. The panels are in Chinese style and are filled with figures of acrobats and tumblers performing actions that make shadows, which form the initials of Hugo and Juliette. It is well known that Hugo took a great deal of interest in the spirit world, particularly after the tragic death of his beloved daughter, Leopoldine. She and her husband drowned in a boating accident shortly after their marriage.

A friend of his, Delphine de Girardin, came to visit him and introduced him to spiritism and table turning. For two years he held regular séances and was a firm believer that he was in contact with the spirit world. He spoke not only to his daughter but also to Joan of Arc, William Shakespeare, and Jean-Jacques Rousseau. The spirits dictated verse to him, which was all in Hugolian style.

During a séance, a friend collapsed in a fit of madness and Mme Hugo soon put her foot down, bringing an end to Hugo's spirit adventure.

Victor Hugo Museum, 6 place des Vosges, 75004, metro St-Paul.

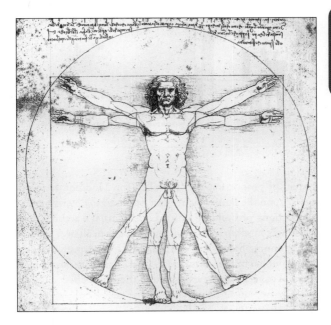

LE CORBUSIER FOUNDATION—ARCHITECTS AND *THE VITRUVIAN MAN*

The Vitruvian Man is an essential part of *The Da Vinci Code*. He is the keystone that links the series of codes that Saunière leaves behind; they send Sophie and Langdon to da Vinci, the painter, but the codes also help them decrypt his use of the Fibonacci sequence. Saunière's body is splayed like a pentacle, directing them to the sacred feminine because the five-pointed star is the symbol of Venus.

The drawing shows man against a framework that illustrates how nature has fitted its creations into the divine proportion of the Golden Mean. Langdon explains this in a lengthy lecture to his students. *The Vitruvian Man* was drawn about 1490 and is named after the Roman architect and theorist Vitruvius, who served under Julius Caesar. His work was of little importance in his day but was of enormous influence from the Renaissance onward.

The Vitruvian Man is the emblem on the Italian one-euro coin. Architects and artists driven by the search for perfection have all sought formulas to achieve this divine proportion. In the 1950s, the architect Le Corbusier advanced a

Nº 85239

FONDATION LE CORBUSIER
10 SQUARE DU DOCTEUR-BLANCHE 75016 PARIS TÉL. 42.88.41.53

LE MODULOR · © F.L.C.

the Modulor designed by Le Corbusier

system of proportion that he called the Modulor. It too is based upon the human figure and was used to determine the proportions of building units. Le Corbusier's architecture, startlingly modern in its own day, can be seen all over France. Two stunning houses in Paris built by Le Corbusier are open to the public; in them his design work, paintings, and architectural conception are exhibited to their best effect.

☞ *Villa La Roche and Fondation Le Corbusier, 8 square du Docteur-Blanche, 75016, metro Jasmin (see map, p. 4).*

SOPHIE AND LANGDON'S LEFT BANK

AMERICAN UNIVERSITY

The American University of Paris was founded in 1962 and is the oldest institution of its kind in Europe. Langdon has come here as one of its prestigious guest lecturers to talk on pagan symbolism at Chartres Cathedral. Before Langdon speaks, he is given the kind of introduction that every lecturer dreads (perhaps it's another personal experience of Brown's).

AUP is an urban institution consisting of a campus of six buildings near the Eiffel Tower and the River Seine. It offers a full complement of liberal arts subjects from anthropology to astronomy, including a complete art history curriculum, though so far it does not include "symbology" in its catalog. As it is an independent college of liberal arts and sciences, it is likely that the course will soon be available!

☞ *American University, metro La Tour-Maubourg.*

THE CLUNY MUSEUM OF MEDIEVAL ART

The Cluny is a must for anyone interested in medieval Paris. Many of the subjects covered by Brown are exhibited in the museum. Few objects of ordinary everyday medieval life have survived, but the treasures belonging to the church were safely guarded. Here you can see relics and reliquary caskets, pilgrim badges, beautiful tapestries, altarpieces, medieval armor as would have been used by the Templars, stained-glass windows, and much more.

The museum contains the tombstone of medieval alchemist Nicolas Flamel and the magnificent tapestry *The Lady and the Unicorn*, subject of another best-seller by Tracy Chevalier. The building itself is medieval and was built about the time Flamel was grand master of the Priory of Sion. By this time the Templars had long been disbanded. The man who built it, Jacques d'Amboise, had the cockle shell of St-Jacques de Compostella as his emblem. You can see this on the stairs of the courtyard of the building, where there is also a "wild man" well and an early sundial. The museum has good facilities, and an excellent book and gift shop.

☞ *The Cluny Museum of Medieval Art, 6 place Paul-Painlevé, 75005, metro Cluny-la-Sorbonne.*

THE COUR DU COMMERCE ST-ANDRÉ AND THE GUILLOTINE

This charming labyrinth of little medieval streets is a marvelous relic of ancient Paris. Le Procope, the oldest café in Paris, is here. Intellectuals and revolutionaries gathered here, many of whom were Freemasons. Remains of the city's most ancient rampart wall can be seen in one of the boutiques in the form of a huge round tower. This wall was built by crusading king Philip

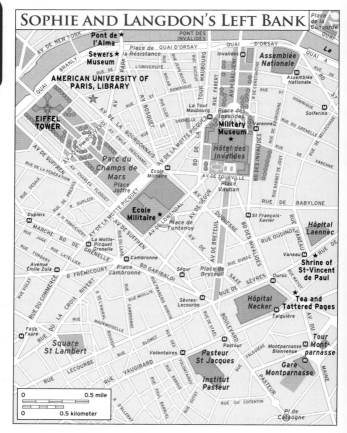

Augustus in the 1180s. This was the time when the split took place between the Priory and the Templars and when Jean de Gisors became Priory grand master.

A plaque is visible showing where Joseph Guillotin invented and perfected the machine that would bring the monarchy in France to its tragic end. It is said that when the king was executed on Concorde Square in January 1793, an unknown man lept onto the scaffold, dipped his hands into the king's blood, and cried, "Jacques de Molay, thou art avenged." A portrait of Guillotin can be seen in the Carnavalet Museum's revolutionary collection. He experimented for two years on lambs, which apparently have necks similar to those of humans. The doctor was a humane man, a Freemason, who sought to find a method of execution that was quick and clean, democratic, and far less barbaric than

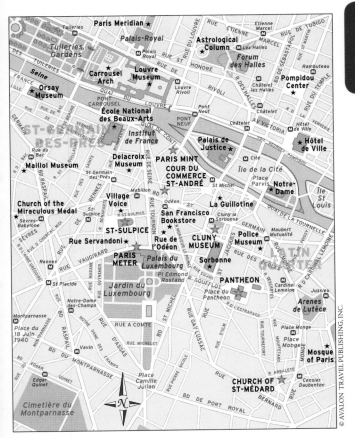

© AVALON TRAVEL PUBLISHING, INC.

methods previously used. In the early days of the Revolution, his invention was given the seal of approval by Louis XVI himself!

The last public execution in Paris was in 1939; the last execution that ever took place was in the courtyard of the Paris prison of la Santé in 1977.

This little street is also lined with many pleasant cafés and tearooms; that is if you have any appetite left.

☞ *Cour du Commerce St-André, metro Odéon.*

ONE RULER REPLACES ANOTHER

At the end of the old city wall, very near the Luxembourg Palace, is the Paris standard meter. This unit of measure was

adopted by the French on August 1, 1793, not long after Louis XVI was beheaded. The meter is one 10-millionth of the meridian arc between the North Pole and the equator.

Until this time, units of measure varied from region to region in France. The metric system, revolutionary in spirit as it was common to all, caused great confusion among the illiterate. Dividing a measure by two, four, or eight had been easy, because any piece of string could be folded in half or into thirds, but to find a fraction of a meter was immeasurably difficult.

Paris standard meter, under the arcades at 36 rue de Vaugirard.

THE MIRE DU SUD

The mire is a stone marker, or bollard, in the parc Montsouris. It measures four meters and is pierced with a small occulus. The name of Napoleon was removed during the Restoration, and a large groove is visible where it was chiseled out.

The mire marks the original Paris meridian, a straight line starting here and running through the center of the Paris Observatory. It joins Dunkerque and Perpignan, passing via the mire du nord in Montmartre. The Greenwich meridian was not adopted until 1884.

To commemorate work done on the meridian by François Arago, France commissioned a work in Paris by the Dutch sculptor Jan Dibbets. This imaginative sculpture consists of more than 100 circular medallions dotted along the meridian line. The first one is by the mire. Each medallion bears the name Arago and has arrows marking the direction of the line. This work replaces the original statue of Arago, which was once situated at the observatory and which was melted down by the Germans during the Occupation.

☞ *Mire du Sud, in the parc Montsouris near the boulevard Jourdan entrance (see map, p. 5).*

The Paris Mint (La Monnaie)

The Paris Mint was built during the reign of Louis XV. It is open as a museum and the story of coins can be traced from their origins to the present day. The huge presses in which coins were struck are on display, and medals are still made here today.

In the courtyard of the museum another gnomon can be seen. It is a vertical meridian in the form of an obelisk like the one at St-Sulpice. Its face is engraved with the 12 signs of the zodiac. The overall height of the obelisk is just under eight meters. The meridian was calculated by a priest called Pingré who had abandoned the church to pursue his passion for astronomy in 1745. The vertical meridian can be seen in the courtyard of the mint when the museum is open.

☞ *The Paris Mint, 11 quai de Conti, 75006, metro Pont-Neuf.*

Pantheon and Foucault's Pendulum

It is an honor to be buried in this church, which has become a monument to France's greatest men. The building is open as a museum and Jean Foucault's pendulum hangs here. (The pendulum inspired a best-selling thriller by Umberto Eco.)

Foucault was a brilliant scientist who specialized in optics. He invented the machine named after him that enabled lens makers to measure focal length precisely. Foucault was determined to demonstrate publicly that the earth rotated. His idea was simple and brilliant. He suspended his pendulum from the dome at about 200 feet. The pendulum has a fine needle point at its base that drags in a sand pit, leaving the trace of its passage. Foucault was able to demonstrate that

MITTERRAND "THE SPHINX" AND HIS GRANDS TRAVAUX

François Mitterrand was president of France for 14 years, 1981–1995. Dan Brown says that he is called the Sphinx in France. He was caricatured as a Sphinx in several leading French newspapers. The name does not derive solely from the pyramid at the Louvre, but from the pharaoh-like nature of his building plan for Paris. Mitterrand's master plan for the city is referred to as his "Grands Travaux." It changed the face of Paris in the 20th century as Haussmann had done in the 19th.

During the 1980s and early '90s, Paris became a huge building site with projects stretching along the Seine from east to west. Monuments such as the Louvre were restored, others, such as the Orsay Railway Station, were reused, and the peripheral areas of Paris were developed from Bercy to la Défense.

Mitterrand is thought to have been a Freemason, member of the Grand Orient Lodge. He also seems to have had dealings with the modern Priory of Sion leader Pierre Plantard de Saint Clair. His visit to Rennes-le-Château before his election was well publicized in France.

The president frequently consulted a famous French astrologer, Elizabeth Tessier, whose job was to calculate auspicious days for his important decisions.

The major buildings of Mitterrand's master plan for Paris from east to west:

Bercy: Ministry of Finance and picturesque wine village. To visit the delightfully renovated wine village go to metro Cour-St-Émilion. Bercy Sports Stadium, pyramid-shaped of course, seats up to 17,000.

The New Bibliothèque Nationale, 11 quai François-Mauriac (see map, p. 5). Four 80-meter towers symbolize open books. Metro Bibliothèque François-Mitterrand.

The New Opera House at la Bastille (see map, p. 53).

The Institute of the Arab World, 1 rue des Fossés-St-Bernard (see map, p. 5). Rooftop tearoom with unbeatable views of Notre-Dame. Metro Jussieu.

The Louvre with its Pyramid Complex, metro Palais-Royal-Musée-du-Louvre.

Complete Refurbishment of the Champs-Élysées, metro Georges-V or Étoile.

The Grande Arche de la Défense, metro Grande-Arche-de-la-Défense. Panoramic lift to rooftop for superb views of Paris. The rooftop terrace is a mosaic of the zodiac called *Map of the Sky*.

the pendulum was stationary and that the earth was rotating. As Dan Brown reminds us, people who had challenged fixed ideas about the universe had been burned as heretics in the past. From the age of Enlightenment onward, even the church had opened its mind toward scientific discovery.

☞ *Pantheon, place du Panthéon, 75005, metro Maubert-Mutualité, open every day.*

PONT DES ST-PÈRES

There are more than 30 bridges in Paris and each one has a story to tell. The pont des St-Pères is where the police catch up with the truck containing the soap bar in which Langdon's GPS dot is hidden. If you ever find this bridge in Paris, please let us know where it is.

THE CHURCH OF ST-MÉDARD

The church is at the bottom end of the lively and bustling market street rue Mouffetard. This lovely church is dedicated to the patron saint of umbrella makers!

In the small cemetery of the church, a strange sect gathered regularly around the tomb of a churchman called François Pâris. Reports of miraculous cures spread rap-

idly, and the members of the sect, called the "Convulsion-ists," would go into trances. The ever-increasing crowds went into a frenzy of collective hysteria. The alarming situation was brought to a sudden end when the church closed the cemetery and pinned a notice in the entrance saying, "The king hereby forbids God to perform miracles in this place!"

Church of St-Médard, metro Censier-Daubenton.

BENEATH
THE
ROSE
LINE

The Story of St-Sulpice:
The Key to the Quest for the Holy Grail

TWO MYSTERIOUS SAUNIÈRES

St-Sulpice is inextricably linked to the mystery of the Holy Grail. A string of endless leads bring researchers back to this church.

The mystery begins when the real-life Saunière, humble parish priest of Rennes-le-Château, found strange coded documents hidden in the pillar of an altar of his church.

He showed them to the bishop of Carcassone, who instructed Saunière to take the documents to St-Sulpice. He spent about three weeks there before returning to Rennes-le-Château, where he then, suddenly and inexplicably, had inexhaustible funds at his disposal. No one has been able to explain his sudden and newfound wealth, although it has been attributed to both alchemy and the illicit selling of Mass. He built a costly road to his church, which was renovated, he built a mansion, which he named Villa Béthanie, and he built a fortified tower to contain his ever-growing library. Coincidentally Béthanie was the name of the arch, or motherhouse, of the Priory of Sion.

Saunière had the inscription "Terribilis est locus iste" or "Dreadful is this place" painted over the porch to his church, which, as will be shown, is another link with St-Sulpice. The second Saunière is, of course, Dan Brown's murdered curator of the Louvre. Saunière from Rennes-le-Château died mysteriously in 1917 on January 17, the saint's day of St-Sulpice.

ST-SULPICE AND A SECRET SOCIETY

A secret society known as the Compagnie du St-Sacrement had its center of operations at St-Sulpice, and the Priory of

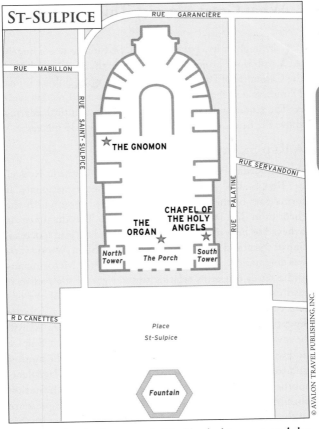

Sion is said to be the power behind both this group and the Knights Templar. An actual abbot named Bieil was here at the end of the 19th century. It is highly likely that he met and had dealings with the priest Saunière, and it is suggested that their dealings were over the hidden treasure. Bieil is the name Brown gives the nun who lives here and acts as the guardian of the Priory's treasure.

The meridian line and the Gnomon, central to *The Da Vinci Code*, are inside the church. (☞ *See* The Gnomon *under* Inside the Church *for a synopsis of the principal events.*)

What Great Mystery This St-Sulpice

Although only a parish church, St-Sulpice was a hugely ambitious project built on a scale that matches that of the Cathedral of Paris. The ground plan of St-Sulpice is just 17 meters less than Notre-Dame, but it is 10 meters wider. The stone vaults of the two are nearly identical, soaring above the heads of the congregation at about 35 meters.

A RED SNAKE

An extraordinary document known as the "Serpent Rouge," or "Red Snake," is kept at the Bibliothèque nationale. It forms part of the famous *Dossiers Secrets* upon which the theories in *The Da Vinci Code* are based. This document is believed to be written by four men, including Jean Cocteau, one of the grand masters of the Priory of Sion. Among various enigmatic texts, such as a genealogy of the Merovingians and a series of poems relating to the signs of the zodiac, it also includes a ground plan of St-Sulpice. One of the poems eulogizes, "Isis queen of all sources benevolent." Isis, the Egyptian mother goddess, is a heroine in the story. As will be revealed, Isis has both a mysterious link with St-Sulpice and with Paris in general. According to this text, the mother goddess Isis is not the Virgin Mary, but Mary Magdalene, mother of all churches. This document reinforces the notion that Mary Magdalene did become a mother. The presence of the genealogy of the Merovingians supports the idea that the authors of the document, whose protectors were at St-Sulpice, believed that the Merovingian kings were the direct descendants of this Mother Mary. The red snake itself symbolizes the bloodline. There seems to be strong evidence that someone wished to suppress the document and the ideas it was perpetuating. The three other men associated with producing it were all found hanged in March 1967. Was this the work of another Silas?

ANCIENT ORIGINS AND A PAGAN PAST

The origins of St-Sulpice date to the 12th century, when as a dependence of the Abbey of St-Germain-des-Prés, the church was dedicated to St-Sulpicius, a 6th-century bishop of Bourges, unsurprisingly of the Merovingian era.

Brown says that a pagan temple dedicated to Isis stood on this ground, and it is also argued that the Celtic founders of the city, the Parisii, took their name from their veneration of Isis. There is plenty of evidence for the many pagan shrines on the Left Bank, dating from the Gallo–Roman period, and maps and drawings from the past do show the existence of this temple, although it was probably closer to St-Germain-des-Prés.

GREAT WEALTH FOR REBUILDING

The church of today is part 17th and part 18th century and was built as a result of this area's suddenly becoming a desirable residential quarter. As Louis XIV prepared to move his court to Versailles, the city naturally spread toward the southwest. Many bridges were built across the Seine to give easier access, and the nobility began to build beautiful mansions on this side of the river. With a new congregation of wealthy benefactors, it became both possible and necessary to rebuild the old church. Anne of Austria, Louis XIV's mother, laid the first stone of the new church on February 20, 1646.

WHERE DID THE MONEY COME FROM?

However, there is perhaps a more sinister explanation for the sudden injection of capital into the rebuilding of the church. It has already been mentioned that the Compagnie du St-Sacrement, a secret society, supposedly empowered by the Priory of Sion, had its center of operations here. It was founded shortly before the rebuilding of the church began, between 1627 and 1629. The men associated with this group include the king's brother, Gaston d'Orleans; Charles Fouquet, the brother of Louis XIV's superintendent of finances; St-Vincent de Paul, the bishop of Alet (a town incidentally near Rennes-le-Château); and Jean-Jacques Olier, the founder of the seminary of St-Sulpice.

SIX ARCHITECTS IN 143 YEARS

This new church was never completed but it stands today as a witness of the architectural audacity and daring of the period. The new style used was both ambitious and remarkable—it was a catalyst that revolutionized the future of Parisian architecture, marking its move toward classicism. The project progressed slowly, troubled by uprisings, (la Fronde) war, and financial difficulties. In the course of building, six architects worked on the church in a period of 143 years!

Rebuilding began at the east end of the church (site of the Lady Chapel and the altar) and work progressed slowly toward the west. After decades of problems, a competition was held in 1732 to find an architect capable of completing the church and its façade. The contract was won by an Italian architect called Giovanni Niccolo Servandoni. He was principally a theater and stage designer, but he had been trained in classical architecture in Florence. His plans were adopted, but when he died in 1766, the work was still incomplete. Servandoni died in a house he had designed next to the church.

The house where Servandoni died can be seen at 6 place St-Sulpice.

Exterior of the Church

☞ *St-Sulpice is located at place St-Sulpice, 75006, metro St-Sulpice (see map, p. 79).*

THE FAÇADE

From the far side of the square, the harmony between the proportions of the façade, the square, and the fountain (19th century) is evident. The façade is both massive and imposing, even more so now that the triangular pediment, originally occupying the space between the two towers, has been demolished. The pediment would have lightened the structure, making it appear less squat than it does today.

GOLDEN NUMBERS

Architects of the ancient world used mysterious formulas to achieve perfection in their designs. Dan Brown explains the use of two of these in his book, the Fibonacci sequence and the Golden Section. These numbers, written by Saunière on the floor of the Louvre just before he dies, reveal the bank account number of his secret safety-deposit box. Mathematicians have demonstrated how the Fibonacci sequence recurs in the most beautiful natural forms, from the perfectly geometrical nautilus shell to the positioning of seeds in a sunflower head. It has been understood and used by man in both art and architecture. The sequence is infinite, in which each number of the sequence is the sum of the two that preceed it—in other words, $1 + 1 = 2$, $1 + 2 = 3$, $2 + 3 = 5$, $3 + 5 = 8$, the sequence being 1, 1, 2, 3, 5, 8, and so on. The increments of the sequence are related to the Golden Ratio, in that, over and above 3, the relationship between any two numbers is 1.618, or that of the Golden Number. This relationship was discovered by the mathematician Robert Simson in the 1750s.

DIVINE PROPORTIONS

The ancients were aware of the Golden Number (called Φ in Greek) and exploited it to create harmonious architectural forms. The visual satisfaction achieved through its use, combined with the unexplainable nature of the number, led Renaissance theorists to believe it was divine.

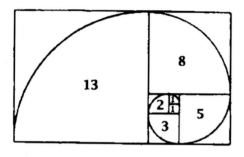

Luca Paciola, a friend of da Vinci, wrote a treatise called *De Divina Proportione* in 1479. This treatise attempts to explain the number, but its title alludes to a belief that this perfection has its source in something far greater than man. The proportion renders a visually satisfying rectangle such as the postcard or credit card. We see this relationship in ordinary everyday objects around us, both natural and artificial, and also in architecture, from the ancient Greek temples to the great classical churches to the modernist constructions of architects such as Le Corbusier. Many artists, including da Vinci, have structured their paintings using this formula. Servandoni would certainly have been aware of this.

DORIC, IONIC, AND CORINTHIAN

Servandoni's design at St-Sulpice translates the Gothic forms of Notre-Dame into a classical two-story portico, flanked by towers. As at Notre-Dame, there are three levels of elevation, three portals, and two bell towers. At St-Sulpice, the cathedral portals with their high pointed gables are arched by semicircular vaults. The rose window of Notre-Dame becomes an Italianate loggia, or balcony, closed in by a colonnade of triumphal arches.

The rose symbolizes the Virgin Mary, and therefore each cathedral dedicated to Notre Dame has one. The lack of such a window may suggest that here it is the Mother Goddess Mary Magdalene, rather than the Virgin Mary, who was considered the more important. This would certainly concur with the arguments in *The Da Vinci Code*. The mas-

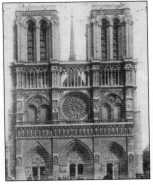

sive square towers of Notre-Dame have been transformed
into circular drums topped with balustrades.

The three stories of the façade follow the classical system
of architectural orders: Doric, Ionic, and Corinthian. The
lower-level columns are Doric, taking their name from the
Greek word meaning "rustic." They are the simplest form,
grooved and slightly tapered toward the capitals on which
lies the entablature. The entablature forms an unbroken
horizontal line that optically reduces the verticality of the
church and harmonizes the relation between its height and
width. Classical architecture aims to create a balanced and
harmonious structure, and each element is carefully calculated to play an important part in the whole. The second
level consists of Ionic columns, again grooved but ending
in scrolls. Originally, the arcaded loggia at this level was
planned to be glassed in to become an enormous library
for the church.

Secret Dossiers and St-Sulpice

Evidently, the church had a large library of books and documents, and it is thought that the elusive Compagnie du St-
Sacrement kept its archives here. The group was to meet
a fate similar to that of the Knights Templar. Its members
were threatened with excommunication by the bishop of
Tours and charged with impious practices in 1651. Eventually, threatened by Louis XIV in 1665, the Compagnie re-
called and concealed all its documents, which were hidden in
a secret depository, thought to be the library of St-Sulpice.
A further literary link between the church and the Priory

of Sion is Victor Hugo. He was married here in 1822 and is named as being grand master of the Priory 1844–1885. Both Charles Baudelaire and the infamous Marquis de Sade were baptized here. The man listed as succeeding Cocteau as grand master of the Priory trained in the seminary here.

MODERNISM WITH A CAPITAL M

This church has a long and complex association with controversial religious thinkers and scholars. In the 19th century, scholars began to apply modernist techniques to biblical scholarship; these looked at the Bible with a new critical methodology. One of the most famous of these was the French writer Ernest Renan, who wrote a controversial *Life of Jesus*. At first, the church embraced this study but soon realized that the Bible could not stand up to the kind of analysis used by this new breed of historian. A conflict ensued and the modernists were soon seen as heretics. One particularly strong voice among this group belonged to Jean-Baptiste Hogan, unsurprisingly the director of the seminary of St-Sulpice 1852–1884.

THE TWO TOWERS—HOME OF ANGELS AND KESTRELS

The two towers are decorated with double pairs of Corinthian columns. The right-hand, or south, tower, which is incomplete, is interesting because it leaves lots of clues as to how the original builders went about constructing the church. The tower is dotted with small hollow cavities that the builders used to plug in their scaffolding. These can be seen on nearly all churches. Sometimes the holes have been plastered in to leave a smooth surface, but here, as at Notre-Dame, they are used even today for maintenance work and so remain visible. On either side of the main opening on the tower there are pilasters (square pillars). These have not been completed, and where the capitals should be there are large bare blocks of stone that protrude, waiting to be carved into acanthus leaves. It can be deduced that the fine details of carving and sculpture were put onto the building in situ by an artist working high on his scaffold. Kestrels nest in the north tower of the church, and there is also a sculptor's studio. The resident artist specializes in carving angels.

THE SACRED TETRAGRAMMATON

 The front of the north tower is decorated with a triangular tympanum, which in turn is carved with the Hebrew tetragrammaton. It is made up of the letters YHWH and represents the never-spoken Jewish name of God, which Jews are forbidden to say so as to guard against desecration of the Sacred Name. In *The Da Vinci Code*, Dan Brown says this name is made up from an androgynous physical union between the masculine *Jah* and the feminine pre-Hebraic name for Eve, *Havah*. He explains that for the ancient Jews, God was seen as having a powerful female counterpart referred to as Shekinah. The Shekinah is also known as the Sabath Bride or Sophia (Chokmah in Hebrew), the goddess of wisdom. Shekinah symbolizes the presence of God and relates to a feminine aspect of the Holy Trinity. It is used to describe the visible manifestation of the divine presence, and is, in fact, another way of referring to God without using his name, for example as God appears to Moses in the burning bush. The sacred tetragrammaton is pronounced as *adonai*, meaning "the Lord," or simply *ha shem*, meaning "the name." This Hebrew inscription is curiously inexplicable on a Christian church. The tetragrammaton, meaning "four letters," is ancient and appears in the Dead Sea Scrolls, which are more than 2,000 years old. Langdon lectures on this to his students.

THE PORCH

It is here that Silas bangs three times on the door in the dead of night to wake up Sandrine Bieil. Standing in the massive porch, he decides to leave his gun behind, thinking it has no place in a house of God. Later, when he murders Bieil, he uses a weapon that the church provides, one of the enormous candlesticks from the altar. As he prepares to enter the church, he believes, without a doubt, that he will soon have the map that will lead his superiors to the location of the secret that will save Opus Dei.

The porch is massive; its width and height seem to dwarf anyone who enters it. The interior is sculpted with seven low-relief panels, illustrating the three theological virtues (Faith, Hope, and Charity) and the four cardinal virtues (Truth, Fortitude, Temperance, and Prudence). They are the work of two brothers called Slodtz, whose work can be seen elsewhere in Paris, including the Church of St-Merry.

A PAGAN INSCRIPTION AND A SUMPTUOUS DINNER

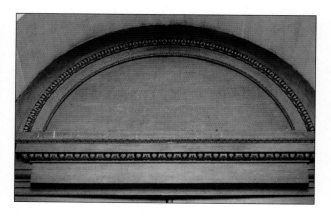

Above the central portal, a faded and enigmatic inscription reads, *Le peuple français reconnoit l'etre suprême et l'immortalité de l'ame.* This translates as, "The French Nation believes in the supreme being and the immortality of the soul." The inscription dates to the French Revolution, when under Robespierre many churches were reopened as pagan temples and used for secular activities. Napoleon once held a banquet here for 750 guests as part of his celebrations on his return from the Egyptian Campaign.

Inside the Church

WINDOWS

In the stained-glass window of the north transept are the intertwined initials P and S. The church maintains that these refer to St-Peter and not the Priory of Sion!

CRYPT

There is a crypt beneath the church where about 5,000 people were buried 1743–1793. Huge trap-doors behind the high altar in the choir were used to lower the bodies into this underground burial chamber. It is said by the church that the revolutionary leader St-Just used to hold secret meetings there.

THE GNOMON

Silas's role at the church centers around the fascinating Gnomon. The Gnomon derives its name from an ancient Greek word that means "indicator," and it is the correct name for the pointer that casts a shadow on a sundial. It is often used to refer to the sundial itself. The Gnomon is in the transept of the building and runs north-south directly in front of the main altar.

MURDER IN THE CATHEDRAL

In *The Da Vinci Code*, Silas has come here for one reason only, to look for the keystone. He has been told that it will lead him to the ultimate treasure. As each of the Priory of Sion masters concurs with his instructions, Silas eliminates him and then comes to the church to seek his treasure. Silas has been told that the coveted keystone lies beneath the Rose Line at the base of the St-Sulpice obelisk. Silas does not realize that he has been tricked.

Sandrine Bieil, guardian of the church, knows that if anyone comes looking for the treasure here, he has infiltrated the innermost ring of the Priory members. She must immediately sound the alert. Silas breaks the floor panel concealing the keystone and finds a tablet containing the disappointing inscription: "Job 38:11." He goes to the great Bible on the altar to read the appropriate passage, and this is when he realizes he has been duped. The passage reads, "Hitherto shalt thou come, but no further." The consequences are terrible. The murders he has commited mean that the secret is lost forever. In a frenzy of rage, the monk discovers Sister Bieil at the phone giving the alert. He uses the candlestick, still in his hand, to carry out her murder.

A MOVEABLE FEAST

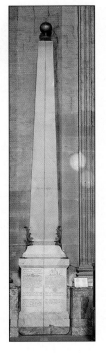

For the purposes of the story, and undoubtedly for dramatic effect, Dan Brown says that the Gnomon is a vestige of the pagan temple that once stood here. Although such an instrument can be construed as pagan, it has both a theological and scientific purpose: An extremely accurate sundial was used to calculate the dates of moveable feasts, such as Easter. It also enabled the astronomer Charles Lemonnier to perfect his observations of the movement of the sun and to study the obliquity of the ecliptic. Many churches were used by scientists for their experiments. Jean Foucault's pendulum is in the nearby Pantheon, and the enigmatic tour St-Jacques was used by Blaise Pascal for perfecting his barometer.

The existing Gnomon was designed by Lemonnier. In 1743, he employed the chief engineer of the Louvre, Claude Lanois, to trace out the meridian line. The original idea dated to 1727, when a Parisian clockmaker decided to create an accurate system by which to set the clocks of Paris.

Markings from this original Gnomon can still be seen on the floor just inside the south transept portal.

The existing meridian line, inlaid in brass, is referred to by Brown as the Rose Line. The term is used to refer to the cardinal points in a compass rose. The Priory of Sion documents do refer to such a line, and the main locations of *The Da Vinci Code* fall on the meridian that runs through St-Sulpice and the Louvre. Brown also assimilates the Rose Line with Rosslyn to lead the treasure hunt of his heroes to the chapel of the same name in Scotland—the Rosslyn Chapel, or the chapel of codes.

Mignonne, Allons Voir Si la Rose . . .

In *The Da Vinci Code* the rose is an extremely important symbol. Teabing and Langdon explain to Sophie how the rose came to reinforce the notion of Mary Magdalene's having produced a bloodline with Christ. The five-petaled rose is like the pentacle of Venus, the goddess of love. We are also told that rose, the same word used in many languages, is an anagram of Eros. The rose symbolizes Mary Magdalene, whose relics are in fact the Holy Grail, and therefore the Rose Line becomes an appropriate indicator or key to the hiding place of this holy secret.

Tempus Fugit

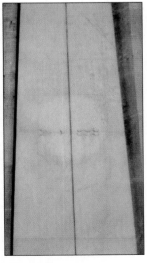

The Gnomon still works but does not function correctly because part of its optical system is now missing. The sundial consists of two lenses in the upper window of the south transept and a marble obelisk in the north. The two are linked by a brass line inlaid into the floor of the church, which is a true north-south meridian. In the floor of the south transept, a carved panel indicates the beginning of the meridian. The meridian ends at the summit of the obelisk; its central point, more or less in front of the main altar, is marked by an oval brass plaque.

During the spring and autumn equinoxes, when the sun is at its zenith and the days and nights are of equal length, the oval plaque is illuminated at midday.

During the winter solstice, when the sun is at its lowest at midday, the light ray falls on the marker of the obelisk.

During the summer solstice, when the sun is at its highest, the south transept floor plaque is illuminated.

Originally the south transept window containing the two lenses was blacked out to reduce light interference. The metal blackout was replaced with leaded glass in 1866. This means that nowadays it is difficult to take clear readings from the Gnomon.

The obelisk, designed by Servandoni, is made from marble and is topped with an orb and cross. Its total height is 10.72 meters. The astrological symbol of Capricorn, ♑, is engraved toward the top. This marks the winter solstice on December 21. Below, on the left side of the brass meridian line, is the sign of Sagittarius, ♐, and on the right side, the sign of Aquarius, ♒. These do not have mystical or astrological significance but are astronomical and denote respectively where the sun marks January 21 and November 21.

The engraved images and texts below give explanations of both the scientific and theological use of the Gnomon. The plinth is engraved on the left side with an array of intertwined scientific instruments, and on the right, with a lamb carrying a cross.

The scientific instruments speak for themselves, and

GNOMON ASTRONOMICUS
Ad Certam Paschalis
Æquinoctii Explorationem

QUOD S. MARTYR ET EPISCOPUS HIPPOLYTUS
ADORSUS EST. QUOD CONCIL. NICÆNUM
PATRIARCHÆ ALEXANDRINO DEMANDAVIT.
QUOD PATRES CONSTANTIENSES ET LATE-
RANENSES SOLLICITOS HABUIT. QUOD INTER
ROMANOS PONTIFICES GREGORIUS XIII.
ET CLEMENS XI. INCREDIBILI LABORE ET
ADHIBITÂ PERITIORUM ASTRONOMORUM
INDUSTRIÂ CONATI SUNT. HOC ÆMULATUR
STYLUS ISTE CUM SUBDUCTÂ LIN. MERI-
DIANÂ ET PUNCTO ÆQUINOCTIALI CERTIS
PERIODORUM SOLARIUM INDICIBUS.

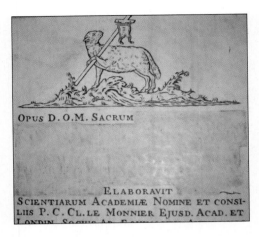

OPUS D. O.M. SACRUM

ELABORAVIT
SCIENTIARUM ACADEMIÆ NOMINE ET CONSI-
LIIS P. C. CL. LE MONNIER EJUSD. ACAD. ET
LONDIN. SOCIUS AB

the lamb is a reminder of Christian sacrifice. Since ancient times, the lamb has symbolized the regenerational power of spring, innocence, purity, and new life. Because it is highly prized, it has often been a principal sacrificial victim. At Easter, it has represented the sacrificial death and resurrection of Christ. John the Baptist, when he first saw Christ, said, "Behold the lamb of God, which taketh away the sin of the world" (John 1:29).

The lamb in the Apocalypse, carrying the book of the seven seals, is Christ as judge at the Second Coming. As the good shepherd, Christ cares for his flock and rescues the lost lamb that has gone astray. Here, the lamb specifically relates to the Gnomon's use by the church for calculating the date of Easter, which falls on the first Sunday after the first full moon that follows the spring equinox. The inscriptions that have been chiseled out referred to the king and his ministers. This was done during the Revolution.

The inscription *Quid Mihi est in Coelo* reflects the Church's use of science. It translates as, "What should I seek in the sky, and what should I desire on earth other than you, Lord, you are the God of my heart and the heritage I desire."

THE CHAPEL OF THE HOLY ANGELS
AND DELACROIX

TERRIBILIS EST LOCUS ISTE

The Chapel des Saints-Anges (Chapel of the Holy Angels) is the first in a series that run along the south-side aisle. It was decorated by Eugène Delacroix between 1861 and 1863, the year that he died. Delacroix, enthusiastic about this project, took a studio near the church; it is now a museum. The paintings have their source in both the Old Testament and the biblical apocrypha. Since they have been known, the latter books became the source for a rich and complex system of images and symbols that became powerful tools for artists.

The ceiling painting shows St-Michael. In Revelations, he is described as the principal fighter in the heavenly battle, casting out the great dragon, and is responsible for the fall of the rebel angel (Revelations 12:7–9). Because his role is primarily military, he is revered by kings and is the patron of knights, soldiers, and armorers. Louis XI founded an order of St-Michael, and Francis I was given Raphael's painting (now in the Louvre), which inspired Delacroix's work here. The order of St-Michael symbolized the union of the king and the church. In the book of Daniel it is said that Michael is the protector of Jacob. Here he watches over his protégé below.

On the east wall of the chapel is the story of Jacob, taken from Genesis 25–37 and 42–50. In his novel *The Nights of Lutetia*, David Shahar shows that he believes that the painting has a hidden purpose: The picture symbolizes the birth of Israel, but it is not clear exactly who Jacob is fighting.

Another curious link exists here with Saunière from Rennes-le-Château, who had the inscription *Terribilis est locus iste* painted above the porch to his church. This comes from Genesis 28:17, meaning "How dreadful is this place." It is what Jacob says after his dream of the ladder and before naming the spot Bethel.

A Remorseful Thief

Jacob, the younger twin, aided by his mother, tricks his brother Esau out of his inheritance. To avoid the wrath of Esau, Jacob spends years in exile. On his return to make peace with his brother, Jacob was attacked in the night. Jacob fought all night with a man who refused to reveal his

identity. At daybreak, he is told he is to be called "Israel," which means "ruling with god." His only wound was a blow to the hip that left him with a limp. At daybreak, Jacob perceives he has been fighting with God.

In the painting, Delacroix draws attention to the immense struggle that Jacob undergoes; every muscle of his body is exaggerated and this is juxtaposed with the calm, statuelike quality of the angel. The painting partly symbolizes mankind's struggle with the upholding of his own religious ideals. The background and the forest are painted with a quick, light, and feathery brushstroke. He was criticized for this but it is an undeniable step toward impressionism. In the foreground, bottom right, there is a small, separate still life. He is said to have painted this in just 20 minutes. Jacob's cloak, arrows, and quiver are represented, as is his straw hat. (The hat is far more likely to have been worn by Delacroix himself than by Jacob.)

A Repentant Sinner

On the west wall, the artist has painted the story of Heliodorus, taken from the second book of Maccabees. The pagan Heliodorus has been sent to sack the temple, but in doing so, he is struck down by an angel on horseback

and dies. The Christians pray for his soul; he is then resuscitated, and he repents and converts to Christianity. This painting is a wonderful vehicle through which Delacroix can exploit his favorite themes: rich oriental colour, textures, jewels, and a horse set against a background of baroque movement. This painting typifies romantic ardor, for which the artist is famous.

Delacroix Museum (last home and studio of the artist), 6 rue Furstenberg, 75006, tel. 01/44-41-86-50, metro St-Germain-des-Prés (see map, p. 79), open 9:30am–5pm, closed Tuesdays.

IF MUSIC BE THE FOOD OF LOVE . . .

The organ of St-Sulpice is considered one of the finest in the world. After having been restored in the 19th century it was reinaugurated. The greatest composers of the day were present, including Camille Saint-Saëns, Luigi Cherubini, Gioacchino Rossini, and César Franck. Some of the finest music ever written, including that of Wolfgang Amadeus Mozart, is shown to follow the rules of the Golden Number. Mozart, Ludwig van Beethoven, and George Gershwin were all prominent Freemasons, according to Brown.

Regular organ concerts are held at St-Sulpice.

UNDER
THE
PYRAMIDS

A Guided *Da Vinci Code* Tour of the Louvre

The proposed circuit in this guided *Da Vinci Code* tour covers some of the museum's most famous works included in the book but also some "off-the-beaten-track" works that illustrate the themes that are evoked in the story. The circuit should take about two hours, but it can be prolonged or shortened depending on whether you hurry or linger.

the Louvre Pyramid

EXTERIOR OF THE LOUVRE

Dan Brown mentions the massive size of the Louvre, which is made up of about eight miles of corridors, and to walk the whole perimeter is a three-mile journey. The building itself, since 1993 one of the largest museums in the world, has been built up through centuries.

Each part of the building echoes art and architecture from differing historical periods. The earliest part of the museum you see is the lovely Renaissance *Cour carrée*, and the most recent is the pyramid. A variety of architectural periods between the two are represented, but the oldest part, the original medieval castle, can be seen only from inside.

Although many traditionalists do not like the modern pyramid, it is appropriate that the museum building, an art-historical manifesto in itself, should also represent the architecture of our own day and age.

The architect I. M. Pei chose the pyramid for several reasons, but primarily he needed to be able to bring light into the underground system of corridors he had designed. This is one of the reasons for the success of his project. Other architects had simply proposed making the unwieldy building bigger. Pei proposed a labyrinth of underground corridors that simplified access to all parts of the museum.

The pyramid has ancient and iconic status in the world of art history and the glass and metallic structure called a *verrière* is a traditional Parisian architectural type. Pei pays tribute to this.

☞ *There is direct access to the Louvre from the metro station "Palais-Royal–Musée-du-Louvre" on line number 1 (see map, p. 21). Leave the metro and follow the platform signs "Musée du Louvre." This will lead you via the shopping mall Carrousel du Louvre to the inverted pyramid. You will pass toilet facilities and a large fast-food cafeteria. The tourist office is near the inverted pyramid. There are security bag checks at this point. As you head toward the main pyramid where you can buy tickets, you pass a post office and the museum's own shops, selling reproductions, museum gifts, and a large book shop specializing in the history of art (many titles are available in English). Bag check-in and cloakrooms are available only after you have bought your ticket. The museum pass is valid here and well worth buying if you are visiting several museums over a few days. (☞ See The Keystone: Paris Practicalities chapter for more information.)*

BENEATH THE PYRAMID

The pyramid complex was opened in 1989 to coincide with the bicentenary of the French Revolution. The renovation of the Richelieu wing, adding 165 galleries and exhibiting 12,000 works, was opened in 1993 to celebrate the bicentenary of the museum.

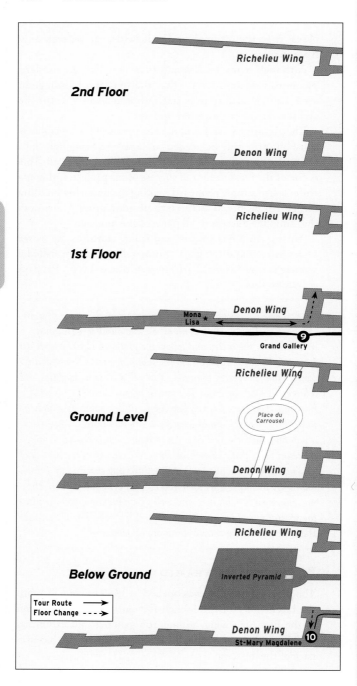

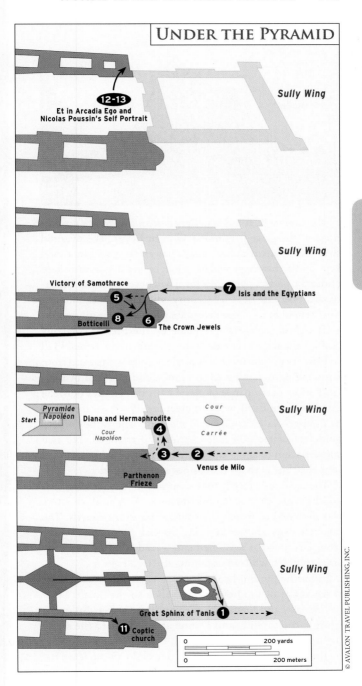

UNDER THE PYRAMID

Sully Wing

12-13
Et in Arcadia Ego and
Nicolas Poussin's Self Portrait

Sully Wing

Victory of Samothrace
5
7 Isis and the Egyptians
8   **6**
Botticelli   The Crown Jewels

Sully Wing

Pyramide
Napoléon

Start

Diana and Hermaphrodite

*Cour
Napoléon*

*Cour

Carrée*

4

3   **2**   Venus de Milo

Parthenon
Frieze

Sully Wing

Great Sphinx of Tanis **1**

11 Coptic
church

0   200 yards

0   200 meters

© AVALON TRAVEL PUBLISHING, INC.

The Louvre pyramid is designed according to the proportions of the great pyramid at Giza in Egypt. The pyramid shape is supposed to have magic powers; it is said that food kept under this shape will keep longer and that a razor kept under the perfect pyramidal form will never go blunt. Unfortunately, because of strict security nowadays you cannot test this, as neither food nor razors are allowed in the museum!

The glass structure was made by the French company St-Gobain, which also made the mirrors in the famed Hall of Mirrors in Versailles. It is made of pure white sand from Fontainebleau, laminated in France, and polished in England. How many panes of glass? Dan Brown says 666, the number of the devil, which is great fun. (☞ *See the* Seven Seals *appendix for the symbolism of this.*) The author of this guide calculates 603 lozenges and 70 triangles. No two sources seem to agree and there has been much ink spilled over this, but perhaps it does not really matter!

The creamy-colored stone comes from the famous Burgundian quarries at Comblanchien. A special concrete was designed to match the color of the stone exactly. The concrete was shuttered using special fine-grained pine from Oregon that was oiled and waxed to give a perfectly smooth finish while maintaining the wood grain.

From the pyramid complex, you can gain access to the three wings of the Louvre: Richelieu to the north, Sully to the east, and Denon to the south. This tour follows a route through Sully and Denon and returns to the starting point.

The entrance ticket is valid all day and you can leave the

museum for a break and return later to take in the Richelieu wing.

Warning! The museum is often obliged to move works
for one reason or another (maintenance, restoration, or for
loan). Pick up the free map-guide from the information
rotunda beneath the pyramid.

ANTIQUITIES

Begin the tour by following the Sully Wing entrance, and
go up the small escalator. At the top, pass the souvenir
boutique, under a minipyramid, and continue to the ticket check. Go straight ahead till you come to the medieval
Louvre. Just before you enter the spectacular moat, there
is a model of the castle and keep (in the wall to the left).
Walk straight on through the moat. The original Louvre
was built by King Philip Augustus in the 1180s to defend
Paris from the English while the king was away on crusade.
The foundations of the castle were discovered and restored
1984–1985. Turn right, following the moat at the corner
tower. This tower is carved with many hearts, which are the
original medieval Masons' marks. Continue through the
moat and pass two towers on your right; these guard the
main entrance into the fortress. A drawbridge, at modern-
day ceiling level, crossed from the castle to the city wall on
your left-hand side. Continue straight, climb the stairs, and
stop at the *Great Sphinx of Tanis*.

THE GREAT SPHINX OF TANIS

Dan Brown's heroes follow
a path coded by symbols
from the ancient world.
Saunière, curator of the
Louvre, collects these symbols, especially the Egyptian ankh. This symbol-
izes the breath of life, and
in Egyptian art, ankh can
be seen held at the nose
of pharaohs by the gods.
The nose was considered

the seat of life by which a magic force entered the body. Invaders later smashed the *Sphinx*'s nose to symbolically take the statue's life. The *Sphinx* is made from one block of pink granite, which comes from Aswan in southern Egypt, but it was found at the delta of the Nile in the north. It weighs 28 tons and was moved using manpower; one man could pull one ton. It was brought to France by boat and the museum had to pierce a hole in the wall to put the *Sphinx* in place. It guards the entrance to the Egyptian collections and is about 4,000 years old.

Take the stairs to your right.

VENUS DE MILO

This is an emblematic work at the Louvre. The statue should really be called *Aphrodite* as she is Greek and not Roman. Her name comes from the Cycladic island where she was found, Melos, which became Milo in French. The name of the island means "apple" and it is thought she may have been holding an apple in her hand. The link between the sacred feminine and the apple is clearly explained in *The Da Vinci Code* and "apple" is the word that opens the final Cryptex. (☞ *See also discussions of symbols in the* Seven Seals *appendix.*)

Venus is thought to be late 2nd- or early 3rd-century BC. Walk along the gallery to look at the statue from a distance. The position she holds is called *contraposto:* Her head is slightly turned, with her shoulders tilted at an angle opposite to the one made by the line of her hips, and one leg moves forward. The right side of her body forms a straight line, the left an S-like curve.

This position, considered lifelike and elegant, is used repeatedly by artists through the ages, and some medieval representations of the Virgin follow this pattern. Later you will see a Mary Magdalene that is inspired by classical Greek sculpture.

Continue along the gallery of Greek antiquities and turn left into the last room, number 7.

PARTHENON FRIEZE

On the far-end wall of the gallery is a fragment of the frieze from the Parthenon Temple on the Athens Acropolis. The frieze formed a continuous band around the top of the building and represented one of the most important annual celebrations of the sacred feminine, that of Athena. Athena was the daughter of Zeus. She is the patron deity of war and also of many skills and crafts, and she is often represented in her armor. Sometimes she has an owl on her shoulder. The procession on the frieze shows just eight out of the original 360 figures that progressed in a stately parade to deliver a woven tunic to the goddess. The solemnity of the occasion is captured in the rhythmic folds of the drapery and the elegant and dignified manner in which the figures stand.

The pattern of the procession is given lively interest by the two male figures who are masters of ceremony. They face the opposite direction, turning toward the young virgins.

As you leave the sculpture, cross the main gallery into the Caryatid Ballroom (room number 17).

ROMAN COPIES OF GREEK STATUES: *DIANA* AND *HERMAPHRODITE*

When the Louvre was still a royal palace, this room was host to the wedding celebrations of the future king, Francis II,

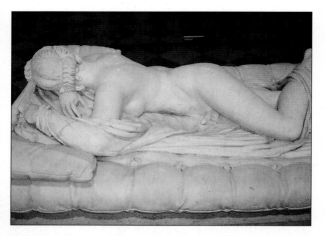

and Mary Queen of Scots. This room is filled with Roman copies of Greek masterpieces.

Many of the original works were made in bronze, but the Romans copied them in marble. The bronze was melted down for use in warfare. Much of our knowledge of Greek art comes from Roman copies rather than the originals, which have been lost. In the middle of the room is the beautiful *Diana*, called the *Diana of Versailles*. She is goddess of the hunt and is associated with the night and therefore is wearing her attribute, the crescent moon, on her head.

At the far end of the room, tucked away in the right-hand corner, is a sleeping *Hermaphrodite*. From behind, the figure looks like a beautiful slumbering Venus; from the front her anatomy leaves no doubt that the figure represents a mythological union of blade and chalice, male and female. The large cushion she sleeps on was sculpted by Bernini in the 17th century. In mythology, the naiad Salmacis prayed that she and the son of Hermes and Aphrodite might be forever united. When she embraced him, their bodies were joined into one, becoming half man, half woman. Biblical Adam is like this until a rib is removed to create a separate female. Some of da Vinci's figures share this same "androgynous" quality. Beside *Hermaphrodite* is a beautiful group representing the three graces.

Leave the ballroom the way you entered, turn immediately right, and then climb the magnificent staircase to *Winged Victory*.

Victory of Samothrace

The *Winged Victory* is another of the Louvre's emblematic goddess figures, one of the most inspired and grandiose of Greek works. The ancients had no complex about using the female figure to symbolize military prowess. Originally the sculpture was painted in bright colors and would have been holding symbols of victory in each hand (probably the laurel wreath and/or a trumpet).

The figure, now headless and armless, was discovered in about 100 pieces. She is believed to commemorate a naval victory in about 200 BC. The ship's prow on which she stands is an original element of its theatrical staging. *Winged Victory* was on a clifftop overlooking the entrance to a harbor.

The grand staircase was built especially for her in the 1930s. Archaeologists found one of her hands in the 1950s, and her thumb is in a museum in Vienna.

Climb the steps left of *Victory* and turn immediately right. This takes you into the rotunda that gives access to the Apollo Gallery.

The Crown Jewels

The Apollo Gallery has just been restored and is home to the collection of curiosities and antiquities that Louis XIV kept at Versailles. The crown jewels from the 17th to 19th century are on display here. The jewelry of Merovingian Queen Aregonde is displayed in the Richelieu wing in the collection of "Medieval Objets d'art."

Leave the Apollo Gallery and turn immediately right. The sixth room, number 30, is part of the Egyptian collection.

Isis and the Egyptians

Cross the room diagonally to the right to find a beautiful collection of statuettes showing the goddess Isis (display cabinet number 2). The theory that Teabing explains to Sophie is wonderfully illustrated here with a collection of small figurines representing Isis breast-feeding her son, Horus.

Isis, her brother-husband, and their miraculously conceived son, Horus, make a Holy Trinity. Their story was retold by the Greeks and eventually by the Christians.

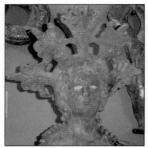

Isis–Aphrodite

Isis

Osiris was murdered and cut into 14 pieces. Isis searched the length and breadth of the Nile and found 13 of the 14 parts, which she miraculously put back together. Not only are they a Holy Trinity but Osiris undergoes martyrdom, death, and resurrection. Horus, with a falcon's head, can be seen to the left.

As you leave the room the way you came in, just to the right of the exit is an *Isis–Aphrodite*; the Egyptian goddess is shown as adopted and adapted by the Greeks (display cabinet number 10). Compare the Greek *Isis–Aphrodite* with the Egyptian goddess next to her.

Walk back to the *Victory of Samothrace*, cross in front of her, and climb the steps to rooms 1 and then 2.

ITALIAN MASTERS: BEHIND *THE DA VINCI CODE*

BOTTICELLI (GRAND MASTER OF THE PRIORY OF SION 1483–1510)

Botticelli is a nickname that means "little barrel." The artist's real name was Alessandro Filipepi. He lived about 1445–1510 and was seven years older than Leonardo da Vinci. The painting in room 2 is a wall fresco from the Villa Lemmi near Florence. It was probably commissioned to celebrate the wedding of Lorenzo Tornabuoni.

In room 1, his wife is presented to Venus and the three graces to prepare for marriage. In room 2, her bridegroom is educated for married life. His education is illustrated by using the symbols of the Trivium and Quadrivium. (☞ *See* Chartres Cathedral *in the* Château Villette and Beyond *chapter.*) A woman, representing Grammar, leads him by the hand to the Trivium. He is presented to a meeting of the liberal arts. Once grammar is learned, he progresses to the other literary subjects: Dialectic holds a scorpion, Rhetoric holds a scroll.

The meeting is presided over by Philosophy, who holds a longbow in the form of a serpent. In the Quadrivium, Arithmetic holds an abacus, Geometry has a set-square, Astronomy has an astrolabe, and Music is playing a portable organ, the bellows of which she is pumping with her left hand.

The grace, delicacy, and linear draftsmanship demonstrated here are typical of the Florentine school. Botticelli has created an atmosphere of melancholy. Comparing the style used here (linear and flat, like a collage) with the painting of da Vinci illustrates what was so special about Leonardo's lifelike way of painting. His figures have an almost photographic reality and literally fit into the perspective of the background.

Continue into room 3, the magnificent *Salon carré*. In this room there are some very beautiful early Italian paintings. On the right as you enter, you will see Giotto's *St-Francis*, the founder of the Franciscan order, receiving the stigmata;

it was painted around 1290. This was during the reign of Philip the Fair, shortly before the downfall of the Templars. The Franciscan rule of simplicity and austerity was similar to the rule adopted by the Templars themselves.

THE GRAND GALLERY: INTRIGUE AND SYMBOLISM

Leave the room by the far door and enter the Grand Gallery, which is where *The Da Vinci Code* intrigue begins. Stand at the beginning of the gallery to admire the fabulous perspective of this great hall. It is here, about halfway along, that "renowned curator Jacques Saunière" is murdered. He tore a Caravaggio from the wall to set off the museum alarm system, and then stripped naked to splay himself like Leonardo's famous *The Vitruvian Man*. He then drew a pentagram on his stomach with his own blood, a clue to the sacred feminine connection. To complete the picture he drew a circle around the circumference of his splayed limbs with a curator's black-light pen. He then wrote the scrambled Fibonacci sequence, followed by, "O Draconian devil! Oh lame saint." Inspector Fache had rubbed out the "P. S. Find Robert Langdon" so that when Langdon sees the crime scene, he is not aware that he is the prime suspect in the murder.

Sophie and Langdon decipher the code. The fact that the numbers are out of sequence is a clue that the letters have also been scrambled. *The Vitruvian Man*, recreated by Saunière's body, leads them to da Vinci. Then the penny drops! The anagram makes "Leonardo Da Vinci, The Mona Lisa." Off Sophie goes to look at the *Mona Lisa*, where she discovers another anagram, "So Dark the Con of Man." This sends her on the trail of *The Madonna of the Rocks*. Behind this painting she finds the key marked P. S. (those letters again!). As Grouard, the security agent, prepares to shoot Langdon, Sophie begins to put her knee through the painting!

The tour continues, though not in the order of the events in the book as the paintings have been moved from their original locations and may well be moved again.

Continue along the Grand Gallery and look out to the left for the Leonardo da Vinci collection. The paintings are hung immediately after the first pair of white marble double columns. (☞ *A short sidebar on life of Leonardo follows the descriptions of his works.*) Here is what you will see.

DA VINCI'S PAINTINGS

JOHN THE BAPTIST

Painted circa 1505–1508. The figure seems quite androgynous, a type of beauty Leonardo had been interested in throughout his life. Some scholars have seen this as an example of ideas that assimilate John to Adam, before the division of the sexes, and as a reinterpretation of the myth of Hermaphrodite. Others see his smile as that of a fallen angel. His fleshy body is unlike the usual image of an adult John, who is usually shown as emaciated after fasting in the desert. Here he is much more suggestive of a pagan god.

THE MADONNA OF THE ROCKS

This painting was ordered by the brotherhood of the Immaculate Conception as the main altarpiece for the newly built Church of San Francesco Grande in Milan. It was painted circa 1485. The picture was never delivered, and a second version was placed in the church; it is now in the National Gallery in London. It is possible that the church rejected the first version because the story that was illustrated was not clear enough. The holy figures have no halos, the angel has no wings, and John the Baptist could easily be confused

with Jesus as he is being taken under the cloak of Mary and does not have his cross-shaped staff. The National Gallery version has all of these symbols, traditionally used to identify the various figures. Art historians have suggested that Leonardo was influenced by heretical ideas, especially those of Amadeo Mendes da Silva. He saw the Old Testament as prefiguring not Jesus, but John the Baptist and Mary, who was assimilated with "Sophia." (☞ *See the* Isis and the Sacred Feminine *appendix.*)

The painting is especially admired for the beauty of the figures, with the delicacy of the sfumato shading technique, perfected by Leonardo, to give them the appearance of living, breathing beings. This work was originally on wood but has been transferred to canvas. (This fact enabled Sophie to start pushing her knee through it to save Langdon from Grouard.)

THE VIRGIN AND ST-ANNE

This is an unfinished work that shows the flow of life between the Virgin, her mother, St-Anne, and the Christ child. This was sometimes shown as the Virgin and Child sitting on St-Anne's knees. Here, the bodies of the two women are almost fused, and it seems as though the Virgin's arm is extended from her mother's shoulder. The Virgin tries to restrain the Child, who is slipping from her arms toward the lamb, the symbol of his sacrifice, from which she cannot protect

him. The beautiful serene face of St-Anne is reminiscent of that of the *Mona Lisa,* as is the mysterious rocky landscape behind the figures.

PORTRAIT OF A WOMAN KNOWN AS *LA BELLE FERRONIÈRE*

Painted circa 1495. This elegant portrait takes its name from the jewel worn across the woman's brow, which was fashionable in Lombardy at the time. Some scholars dispute that the work is by Leonardo and although the woman was once thought to be the mistress of Leonardo's patron Ludovico Sforza, this is now questioned. Her perfect oval face is characteristic of the Italian Renaissance ideal, but her enigmatic gaze, glancing to the right as she seems to turn toward the viewer, gives this work a special depth. The reflection of her red velvet dress in the warm glow of her cheek is particularly lovely.

HOMAGE AND RESURRECTION

Farther along the gallery there is a superb portrait by Raphael of *Baldassare Castiglione.* He wears a hat and has a long beard. The portrait is a homage to the *Mona Lisa.*

You will pass a painting by Bronzino, *Christ apparaissant à*

BIOGRAPHY OF LEONARDO DA VINCI (1452–1519)

Leonardo da Vinci was the illegitimate son of a lawyer and a woman about whom little is known. He was born near the town of Vinci and spent several years in the care of his grandmother, which has led people to speculate that he fused St-Anne and the Virgin in the painting of this name because for him, grandmother and mother were one. When he was a child he had a dream that a bird of prey descended on him in his cradle. It opened his mouth with its tail feathers and moved them about between his lips. He took this as a sign that nature wanted to speak to men through his mouth. It was a dream he never forgot. Sigmund Freud saw the shape of this bird of prey in the figure of the Virgin's robe in the painting of the Virgin and St-Anne.

He was apprenticed to Verrocchio in Florence at the beginning of his career as an artist. Verrocchio was fascinated by mathematics, alchemy, and magic, and his studio was the center of the most modern ideas of its day. Leonardo was remarkably beautiful, courteous, a bit effeminate, and a loner. He had difficulty finishing his projects and paint-

Madeleine. This shows Christ appearing to Mary Magdalene after the Resurrection. She is the first to see him and mistakes him for a gardener. Christ says, "Noli me tangere," which means, "Touch me not." He goes on to say, "But go to my brethren and say to them I ascend unto my father."

CARAVAGGIO: *THE FORTUNE TELLER* AND *THE DEATH OF THE VIRGIN*

Several Caravaggios are in the gallery and which one Saunière throws to the ground is not specified. In the light

ings. Once he had solved an idea he wanted to move on. Leonardo was not highly educated, but he was interested in everything and excelled in many disciplines. Like others in his time, he was intrigued by irrigation, hydraulics, and war machinery, and he was also an accomplished musician. He wrote extensively on the theory of art, was fascinated by riddles and enigmas, and made extensive notes in a special script, which, as he was left-handed, he called his "mirror writing." His contribution to art is to have produced the most beautiful figures representing feminine spirituality. He brought to perfection the "sfumato" style of gentle contours, in which the figure is bathed in a soft light, making it look at one with its surroundings.

Leonardo worked for patrons such as Lorenzo the Magnificent in Florence, Ludovico Sforza in Milan, and was eventually invited to France at the end of his life by King Francis I. He was given a mansion and a pension by the French king so that he could live comfortably, at the royal town of Amboise in the Loire Valley. Nothing was required of him except the pleasure of his conversation. Leonardo died and was buried in Amboise in 1519. The *Mona Lisa* seems to have been a favorite painting and he did not wish to part with it during his lifetime.

of his own devotion to Mary Magdalene it would be appropriate if it were *The Death of the Virgin*, but this huge canvas would be somewhat unwieldy! *The Death of the Virgin* scandalized the church because the artist had painted the scene with too much realism. He was accused of using a dead prostitute, fished out of the River Tiber, as a model. During this period, people were used to seeing the Virgin represented elegantly clothed, sitting on a cloud and being transported up to heaven.

Another beautiful painting by this artist is *The Fortune*

Teller. It shows a wealthy young man having his palm read while the gypsy fortune teller is stealing his ring.

Caravaggio died at 37 having lived a tempestuous life. He killed a man in a brawl and died in a fit of rage. His paintings make bold use of chiaroscuro (the heightened contrast of light and dark), which adds drama to the scenes.

Continue along the gallery toward the *Mona Lisa.*

TO DA VINCI'S *MONA LISA*

Painted on a poplar wood panel circa 1504, sometimes called *Portrait of Mona Lisa del Giocondo* (hence the title *La Joconde* in French). Langdon mentions that her name is an anagram of Amon L'Isa, the divine union of male and female. This, he says, is the reason for her smile. It would seem that the work started as an actual portrait of the young wife of del Giocondo. Leonardo's biographer Giorgio Vasari writes of how singers and musicians were employed to entertain her while she modeled to make her expression less melancholy. However, despite these details, it would seem that the portrait is of an ideal and not a specific person. The pyramidal structure of the composition accentuates her brow, the seat of the intellect. The simplicity of her tunic and her loose hair under a delicate veil give the figure a timeless appeal and leave room for the imagination. This is in contrast to the way portraits at the time generally show the status of the sitter by fashionable clothes and an elaborate interior. Her smile is extremely delicate, one of interior meditation.

In the background is a mysterious rocky landscape, with the imprint of man in the form of a road and a bridge (the winding path represents the journey of the soul). In the distance, the landscape is completely wild.

As Langdon points out, the horizon seems to be different on the left and the right of the figure. The reason for this is open to interpretation. The strokes of the paintbrush are so delicate that they cannot be seen.

After visiting *Mona Lisa,* walk back to the large-format French paintings. Some of the museum's most famous 19th-century works are here, including: Théodore Géricault's *Raft of the Medusa* and Eugène Delacroix's *Liberty Leading the People.* Continue to Paolo Veronese's *Wedding at Cana.*

WEDDING AT CANA

Veronese's *Wedding at Cana* is the largest painting in the Louvre. In *Da Vinci Code* theory, the wedding taking place is really between Christ and Mary Magdalene. In this version, Christ and the Virgin Mary (the mother-in-law?!) sit in the center of the painting, and there are a bride and groom present (can you pick them out from the crowd?).

The painting was commissioned by the Benedictines of San Giorgio in Venice as a decoration for their refectory, and it was delivered in 1563. One imagines the monks having their meagre meal with this sumptuous banquet taking place behind them. The painting immortalizes the first of Christ's miracles, when water is turned to wine. The 132 figures were painted in less than a year and the picture is rich in religious symbolism. The horizontal balustrade separates the terrestrial sphere from the heavens. Above Christ's head, between the posts of the balustrade, is a pilgrim's bottle, symbolic of the water that Christ turns to wine. Lamb is being carved above Christ's head, which represents Christ as the sacrificial lamb even at the time of his first miracle. Beneath Christ is an hourglass, showing that time is running out and that the end of Christ's life approaches. The hourglass looks like an image of the Holy Grail. Beneath this, two dogs chew at a bone, the symbol of death. The two dogs are chained together and one wishes to pull away but can't: This symbolizes marriage!

High up on the right-hand side, a hand throws carnations to earth from heaven. The name for this flower refers to the Incarnation (Christ's becoming flesh) and its red color symbolizes the Crucifixion. Many dogs are in the painting, including one up in the heavens that looks straight at Christ. Dogs are often used to symbolize loyalty

and fidelity, which suits a marriage scene. Here, they are also believed to represent the creature to whom we throw terrestrial nourishment, which is in contrast to the spiritual nourishment offered by Christ.

Veronese's self-portrait is said to be that of the viola player, and the master of ceremonies pouring the wine is his brother Benedetto.

Other painters are thought to be portrayed here: Titian plays the contrabass, Tintoretto the violin, and Bassano the flute.

Walk back the way you came, to the end of the large-format gallery, go down the stairs marked "escalier Molien," and at very bottom of the steps take a sharp right turn; go down again, following "entresol" and "12th to 16th century Italian sculptures." Turn right into the Northern Sculpture room.

St-Mary Magdalene

At the entrance to room C is a beautiful carved and painted wooden statue of Mary Magdalene by the German artist Gregor Erhardt. Here she is shown naked with long flowing hair. This symbolizes Mary at the end of her life when she was living the life of a repentant hermit. The back of the sculpture contains a door to a small compartment.

At the far end wall there are two carved wooden altarpieces; the smaller one on the right-hand side illustrates episodes from the life of Mary Magdalene in lively sculptures, and the larger one shows a scene of the Crucifixion. Mary Magdalene is at the foot of the cross with her alabaster jar of ointment.

Return to room 3, turn right, and walk through Italian and Spanish sculptures. Opposite the exit as you leave, there is a beautiful primitive Italian tetramorph. Go down the steps, cross the hall, and go up the steps into pre-Classical Greece.

Ancient and Sacred Texts

In room 1 of pre-Classical Greece, you see some very ancient idols, including the *Bell Shaped Idol.*

Continue through the gallery to room 3, turn right into room B, and follow the sign down the steps into room C. Here you will find yourself inside the reconstruction of a Coptic church.

This room was once the amphitheater of the Louvre school and has been reserved to house the generous gift from Egypt, the fragments of the monastery church of Baouit. A scale model of the monastery stands in the middle of the room.

This site was excavated from middle Egypt by French archaeologists and dates from the 4th to the 12th centuries.

The Coptic Church is the Christian church in Egypt. It is based upon the teachings of Saint Mark, who brought Christianity to Egypt in the 1st century AD.

The Nag Hammadi texts, found in upper Egypt in 1945, are bound manuscripts and are written in the Coptic language, which is still used by Coptic Christians in Egypt. These are the books known as the Gnostic Gospels.

The Dead Sea Scrolls are written in Hebrew and Aramaic and were the records of an ascetic sect known as the Essenes. This sect lived at around the time of Jesus and John the Baptist. The Nag Hammadi texts, or Codices, were written slightly later and were copied into Coptic from the Greek originals. The Coptic Church uses the looped cross called the Crux Ansata. This comes from the pagan Egyptian ankh. Paganism was still a strong force in the early Christian period. Back in room B, a small display cabinet labeled "Magie" shows handwritten spells and incantations, along with some lucky charms and figurines that have been stuck with pins like voodoo dolls.

Walk back through pre-Classical Greece and return to the pyramid. Your tour can finish here. Leave the pyramid, following the metro signs, if you wish to see the inverted pyramid.

If you want to go into the Richelieu wing, you can see two more paintings that are an important feature of the book *Holy Blood, Holy Grail.*

NICOLAS POUSSIN

ET IN ARCADIA EGO

On the top floor of the Richelieu Wing, 14th–17th century French paintings, room number 14, you'll find *Et in Arcadia Ego (The Arcadian Shepherds)*, painted circa 1640.

This is one of Poussin's best-known works. A group of shepherds and a classically dressed woman in the idyllic land of Arcadia come across a tomb on which they decipher the inscription "Et in Arcadia Ego," which means, "Even in Arcadia I (Death) Exist." One of the shepherds kneels beside the tomb and traces the inscription with his finger. This reminds them that death is present even in what seems to be paradise. The man and the woman on the right are discussing the idea, while the man on the left is absorbed in meditation.

This is an allegorical painting and has the same message as a "vanity" painting, which emphasizes the ephemeral quality of human life, as does the shadow of the shepherd who reads the inscription. There is no moral. The painting has a mood of elegiac poetry and was intended to provoke a meditation on human frailty. Paintings on this theme often depict Mary Magdalene meditating with a skull or an oil lamp, the symbol of repentance. There is a beautiful painting by George de la Tour on this theme in the Louvre.

The mysterious manuscripts found by Saunière at Rennes-le-Château make coded references to both *Shepherds* and Poussin. The authors of *Holy Blood, Holy Grail* claim to have found the tomb and the landscape that figure in Poussin's painting *The Arcadian Shepherds*. It is at Arques, near Rennes-le-Château.

SELF-PORTRAIT

This sensitive work, painted in 1650 and in the same room as *The Acadian Shepherds*, shows Poussin in a philosopher's gown, with slightly unkempt hair and a troubled look, surrounded by paintings, mostly hidden from view, and holding a portfolio of his drawings.

The work can be compared to other artists' self-portraits in which they are glorified and surrounded by the attributes of the arts to emphasize their many intellectual achievements.

Here Poussin shows only one detail of his work, which is emphasized for symbolic reasons: a woman in profile with a headdress decorated with one eye. She represents the art of painting, and the two outstretched arms that embrace her may represent Poussin embracing his profession or his friendship for the man who commissioned the work. Poussin is wearing a ring with a diamond cut into a four-sided pyramid, a common Stoic symbol of constancy. Poussin was not interested in portraiture and was going to have the work done by another painter, but he finally decided to paint it himself, thinking no one else would produce a painting to his satisfaction.

CHÂTEAU
VILLETTE
AND
BEYOND

Château Villette

Château Villette is the magnificent property near Paris where Leigh Teabing lives. He lives the expat's dream life, having built himself a little England within the bounds of his French château. The actual château that inspired Brown is called the château de Villette and it is near Pontoise in the heart of "impressionist" countryside. It was built by the prestigious architect François Mansart for the count of Aufflay, who was Louis XIV's ambassador to Italy. Mansart had built some beautiful mansions and town houses in Paris, including his own, which can be seen at 5 rue Payenne in the Marais. This extraordinary building became the headquarters of the curious cult of positivists. This is the only positivist meetinghouse in France and is the location of their Chapel of Humanity. No supreme being is worshiped here; members meditate upon great men of the past: Dante Alighieri, William Shakespeare, René Descartes, Homer,

château de Villette

Aristotle, and Julius Caesar. Their motto, "Love as a principal, order as a basis, progress as a goal," is written on the front of the building. Mansart built his home here in 1622. He is also remembered for building the magnificent dome of the oratory of the Val-de-Grace in Paris.

The château de Villette was finished in 1696 by Jules Hardouin-Mansart, the architect's grandnephew, who also built the Hall of Mirrors at Versailles for the Sun King. The gardens of the château de Villette are typical of the formal French style of Le Nôtre, with lovely lakes. They are appropriately home to an obelisk and a pair of sphinxes.

FAMOUS PEOPLE AT THE CHÂTEAU DE VILLETTE

In the 18th century, the château was owned by the Marquis de Grouchy. His daughter was married in the chapel here, and her name was Marie Louise Sophie. Her husband was Condorcet, a political theorist whose ideas were remarkably modern. He was a moderate in the Revolution and supported the idea of giving women the right to vote. His close friend La Fayette was a witness at the wedding. The story told at the château is that M. L. Sophie and La Fayette fell in love at first sight, but La Fayette, unable to be disloyal to his friend, left France with a broken heart for America. Apparently the lovely Sophie wasted no time in replacing him. Condorcet and La Fayette were both Masons and held frequent Masonic meetings here. During the

Revolution, Condorcet, promoter of free education for all and contributor to the great French *Encyclopaedia*, took his own life rather than be sent to the guillotine.

FAMOUS FACES FROM MODERN TIMES

The château is no stranger to the silver screen. Many films have been made here, including *The Count of Monte-Cristo*, starring Gérard Depardieu, and *Le Libertin* with Fanny Ardant. It is also making an appearance in the film based on *The Da Vinci Code*.

Today the château is privately owned and has been beautifully restored and furnished. It is available for visits, weddings, and conferences. The present owner, Olivia Hsu Decker, organizes special *Da Vinci Code* holidays. These include staying in the luxurious accommodations offered at the château and gourmet food.

For more information and booking, local contact is Andrew Ryan, tel. 06/64-81-12-48, andrew.ryan@laposte.net; or U.S. tel. 415/435-1600, fax 415/383-1258, villette@ frenchvacation.com.

Other Local Curiosities

THE MUMMIFIED LEG OF MARIE DE MEDICI

The Musée Tavet in Pontoise exhibits an eclectic collection of curios. Both local history and modern art fill its galleries, but deep in the heart of its storerooms is the mummified leg of the queen. The relic was saved during the revolutionary destruction of the royal tombs at St-Denis. It was later acquired by a Mr. Tavet, a historian and scholar. He founded the museum and is its principal legator. When he died in 1892, his personal collection was donated to the museum. This included the leg of the queen. This fragile relic is not on general view.

☞ *The Musée Tavet-Delacour, 4 rue Lemercier, 95000 Pontoise, open 10am–12:30pm and 1:30–6pm Wednesday–Sunday.*

ÉCOUEN

Not far from Paris is the beautiful Renaissance château d'Écouen. The home was built for the head of the king's army, Duke Anne de Montmorency.

The collections here are fascinating and include the famous set of 16th-century tapestries telling the story of David and Bathsheba. *The Dying Slaves* by Michelangelo once adorned the façade of the inner courtyard. Many beautiful frescoes are here, as is a superb collection of Renaissance objects and furniture.

The most extraordinary exhibit is an exact replica of Leonardo da Vinci's *The Last Supper*, which is in the family chapel. This painting is of inestimable interest because although a copy, it is a contemporary work and probably the best representation anywhere of what da Vinci's painting originally looked like.

THE DA VINCI CODE:
TEABING INTERPRETS *THE LAST SUPPER*
Having explained to Sophie that the Holy Grail is actually Mary Magdalene, Teabing uses the following arguments from the painting to support the theory: Each of the disciples

has an individual wineglass; the chalice or cup, as described in the Bible, is not being passed among the grouped figures. The figure to the right of Christ is analyzed as being a woman, with "flowing red hair, delicate folded hands, and the hint of a bosom. It was, without a doubt . . . female." Teabing tells Sophie, "That, my dear, . . . is Mary Magdalene." The two central figures wear inversed clothing and represent yin and yang (the concept of masculine and femine being both essential parts of a whole). The space between them forms a V shape, symbol of the chalice or sacred feminine. The two figures, if seen as a whole, form a large letter M, which stands for Mary Magdalene, the Grail that is present after all. Teabing argues that Christ in fact entrusted his church to Mary Magdalene. Because of this, Peter, who was jealous, makes a cutting gesture at her throat. Teabing also describes a mysterious disembodied hand holding a knife.

☞ *Écouen is accessible by train from Paris–gare du Nord. Journey time to Écouen–Ezainville station is about 25 minutes. The walk from the station to the château is a leisurely half hour. The museum is closed on Tuesdays.*

LE BOURGET

Teabing keeps his private jet here and makes a quick getaway with a stifled Silas bound and gagged in the back of the plane. It is here that they make their first attempts to open the Cryptex.

Le Bourget was once a place of magic where the pioneering "magnificent men in their flying machines" would experiment. In the 1930s, rich and fashionable jet-setters would fly into Paris via Le Bourget airfield. The Golden Age of romance is long gone, and Le Bourget is today swallowed up in Paris's ever-growing suburbs. Today it is home to the Museum of Flight and Space Travel. Its horizon is dominated by the French rocket *Arianne*. The Anglo–French Concorde is part of the museum and can be visited here.

THE *SPIRIT OF SAINT LOUIS*

On May 21, 1921, Charles Lindbergh landed at Le Bourget at 10:22pm. After 33.5 hours of flight he completed the first-ever Atlantic crossing. This exploit had created enormous excitement in Paris, and it is reported that 100,000 people were there waiting for him when he arrived. The French rewarded his incredible achievement by giving him the prestigious Legion of Honor.

☞ *Museum of Flight and Space Travel, Aéroport du Bourget BP 173, 93352 Le Bourget Cedex.*

☞ *If you wish to visit Paris in the* Spirit *of Langdon and Sophie, contact Paris Helicoptere for a ride, departure from Le Bourget every Sunday, for a 25-minute tour of Paris, at tel. 01/48-35-90-44, or try Montgolfière Aventures for a more sedate visit but a bumpier landing, tel. 01/40-47-61-04.*

Chartres: The Town and the Cathedral

Langdon has come to Paris to lecture on the pagan symbolism of the cathedral. It was originally a pagan holy shrine and like many other churches, it is built on an ancient holy well. There is much to see here and it is worth planning to spend a whole day. Both the cathedral and the medieval town are beautiful. You can climb to the roof of the cathedral for superb views across the city's rooftops and the magnificent plains of the Beauce region. The town is bustling and there are plenty of restaurants and cafés for lunch. The local speciality is the Mentchikoff, a truffly chocolate coated in meringue. These are sold in attractive boxes illustrated with a picture of the cathedral.

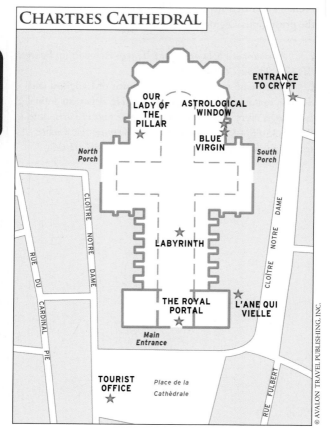

Chartres is about 55 miles southwest of Paris. It is easily accessible by train from Montparnasse Station, and the journey takes about an hour. On arrival at Chartres, go straight to the tourist office and ask for a free map, which includes a guided tour of the old town. Headphone commentary can be rented to accompany the visit. Guided tours of the cathedral are given in English by local specialist Malcolm Miller. Ask for the tour program at the tourist office.

A GUIDED TOUR FOR PAGANS AND CHRISTIANS

Chartres Cathedral

At Chartres, legend, myth, and history mix to make the story that has come down to us today. The holy site has pagan origins and the first church here was built above the pagan well. It is said that pre-Christian Druids practiced a virgin cult here.

There is evidence of a church's being destroyed and rebuilt here as early as 743 AD. Toward the end of the 8th century, Pepin the Short, Dan Brown's insecure Merovingian shorty, made a gift to the church of "Mary at Chartres." The city and church were sacked in the 9th century. A new church was built and consecrated in 876, and it was at this time that Chartres acquired its precious holy relic, the Sancta Camisia. This veil, which is on display inside the church, is purported to have been worn by the Virgin Mary when she gave birth to Christ. At a time when the cult of the Virgin was gaining importance in Europe, this relic was a valuable asset capable of generating income for the church. It was also valuable protection for the city. When the Viking Rollon came to besiege the city, the veil was displayed before him; he and his men fled, then made peace, and converted to Christianity. These men would become the great cathedral builders of Normandy, who gave their names to the Norman style of architecture.

Through the 10th and 11th centuries, Chartres became an extremely important and active center of learning, and it remained so until the Sorbonne was founded in Paris. In the early 12th century, neo-Platonist Bernard of Chartres was one of the famous scholars. He saw the scholars of his time as dwarves perched on the shoulders of giants. The giants were the philosophers of the ancient world. This theme is reflected in the decorative scheme of the façade.

Medieval education was divided into the seven liberal arts. These were divided into two subgroups, respectively the Trivium (three-branch) and the Quadrivium (four-branch). The mind was seen as being enlightened by the Quadrivium (mathematics, geometry, astronomy, and music) and as expressing itself through the Trivium (grammar, rhetoric, and dialectic). These are all represented on the royal portal of the cathedral.

THE ROYAL PORTAL (1145–1155)

These are the oldest statues and carvings at Chartres. The royal portal is divided into three bays.

CENTRAL PORTAL

The tympanum shows Christ the teacher in a *mandorla* surrounded by the tetramorph. (☞ *See the* Glossary *under the* Inside the Cryptex *appendix.*) The tetramorph represents the evangelists who spread the teaching of Christ. The gesture Christ is making with his right hand signifies that he is speaking, and the book in his other hand shows that he is speaking about the Bible, in other words, teaching.

RIGHT PORTAL

The tympanum shows Christ as a child with the Virgin Mary. Beneath this, on the lintel, is the Presentation at the Temple, and beneath this, the Nativity. A shepherd in medieval stockings plays the panpipes while standing over his flock of archaic sheep.

Two ribbed archivolts surround the tympanum. The figures here represent the Trivium and Quadrivium. At

the base of the inner archivolt, on the right-hand side, sits Pythagorus, and on the outer, Donatus. Above Pythagorus, Music plays bells, and above Donatus, Grammar beats her lessons into boys with a birch stick. On the outer archivolt, on the left-hand side, at the bottom, is Aristotle.

On the sculpted capitals wrapped around the buttress between the central and right-hand portal is a lovely carved Last Supper, and just right of this is the Kiss of Judas.

LEFT PORTAL

The tympanum shows Christ's ascension. Beneath this can be seen beautiful flying angels. In the archivolt, one can see the labors of the month and the signs of the zodiac: starting at the bottom outer left is harvesting in July and above the harvest is the sign of Cancer. At the bottom inner right is smelling flowers in spring, and above this is the symbol of Aries the ram. The complete zodiac can be followed all the way around the portal.

South Portal, left-hand bay: a carving of medieval knights beheading Thomas à Becket

In the left-hand bay is a carving of medieval knights beheading Thomas à Becket.

HOLY WELL

This is in the crypt and is 33 meters deep; it was undoubtedly the original Gallo–Roman well.

ISIS AND THE CULT OF BLACK VIRGINS

There were two black Virgins at Chartres, but only one has survived. "Our Lady of the Crypt" was destroyed in the Revolution, but "Our Lady of the Pillar" is in the chapel at the angle of the choir and the north transept. The statue is made from painted pear wood and is probably from the 16th century. There are many of these statues in the south of France, and their origin is unknown. It is argued, however, that the black Virgin statues descend from the cult of Isis. The Virgin's crown of stars and association with water are both borrowed from the iconography of Isis.

L'ANE QUI VIELLE

Outside the cathedral on the south side is a sculpture of a donkey playing a hurdy-gurdy. It is in poor condition and its symbolism remains obscure.

AN ANCIENT LABYRINTH

Just inside the cathedral is the beautiful and mysterious labyrinth. There were labyrinths like this in many cathedrals, including Sens, Amiens, Arras, and Reims. These were later removed because they were considered pagan. A labyrinth is defined as being the longest possible route in the shortest possible space. Here the line is several hundred meters long and pilgrims arriving here on the route to Compostella would crawl along the line, saying prayers on their hands and knees. It takes about an hour to complete this journey. It is also referred to as "the road to Jerusalem," but for the pagans, it was the journey of life ending in death. For the Christians, at least paradise was waiting at the end.

CORPORATIONS AND SECRET SIGNATURES: THE WINDOWS

Each window at Chartres was given by a wealthy local corporation and includes the guild signature in the lower corners of the windows. These are fairly easy to identify. The Mary Magdalene window (second window in the south-side aisle) was given by the water carriers, and they can be seen in the bottom left- and right-hand corners of the window. The water carriers have an affinity with Mary because she washed Christ's feet with her tears. The Good Samaritan window (third in the south aisle) was given by the shoemakers. They can be seen in their workshops in the bottom three panels of the window. The shoemakers of Chartres were very wealthy, as the pilgrims arriving on foot had to buy new footwear. Walk round the church to the north-side aisle; starting at the first window, nearest the façade, you'll see coopers, carpenters, and wheelwrights; second window, wine merchants; third window, drapers and furriers; fourth window, bankers; fifth window, haberdashers and apothecaries; and sixth window, blacksmiths.

THE FAMOUS BLUE VIRGIN OF CHARTRES

This can be seen in the first bay of the south side, after the transept crossing. This window is a relic of the ancient church; it was found in the debris after the fire of 1194. Having survived the fire, the window was considered miraculous. It was paraded as a religious relic, along with the Sancta Camisia, to raise money for the rebuilding

of the church. The 12th-century panels were set in a new window. Two different colors of blue are apparent; the lighter 12th-century blue is the famous "blue of Chartres." (☞ *See illustration on page 147.*) The Sancta Camisia is visible in a side chapel.

The Astrological Window next to the Blue Virgin

This window was donated by both the vine-growers and Count Thibault of Champagne. Signs of the zodiac are shown in the medallions on the right, and the corresponding labors of the month are on the left. The central medallions show both a sign and the seasonal labor. January is shown with three heads, looking at the past, present, and into the future.

The west-façade windows, beneath the main rose, are, from left to right: the Jesse Tree, the Incarnation, the Passion, and the Resurrection.

The west rose tells the story of the Last Judgment.

Chartres Cathedral

Rennes-le-Château

At the heart of the mystery on which *The Da Vinci Code* is based is the ancient hilltop town of Rennes-le-Château. The story of the Abbé Saunière and his mysterious finds is told in detail in *Holy Blood, Holy Grail* by Michael Baigent, Richard Leigh, and Henry Lincoln. This book should be on the reading list of anyone interested in the issues raised in *The Da Vinci Code*. The town is in the Aude region of France, famous for its associations with the Cathars and Templars. At Rennes-le-Château, the principal sites open to the public are: the village, the church of Mary Magdalene with its strange carvings and inscriptions, and Saunière's house. Waxwork figures made by Alfred Grévin and several other curios can be seen, including a neolithic carved sacrificial altar and a carved stone slab known as the Knights' Stone. The Wisigothic pillar in which Saunière found the hidden documents is on display, as is a special hollow lectern with a secret cavity. The Magdala tower and Saunière's private chapel are also open.

☞ *Check with the tourist office (www.rennes-le-chateau.fr) before planning a trip to Rennes-le-Château. Opening hours vary and are reduced during off-peak seasons.*

THE
KEYSTONE:
PARIS
PRACTICALITIES

MUSEUMS

Most museums in Paris are closed either Mondays or Tuesdays.

MUSEUM PASS

The museum pass is a good value if you wish to visit two or more museums in a day, and it is valid for one, three, or five days. The pass is available at major metro stations and most museums. It gives priority entrance to permanent collections but does not include temporary exhibits. You may buy it in advance and it is validated as of your first museum visit.

Some museums are free the first Sunday of the month. Many museums are free for under 18s (bring ID).

ART AND HISTORY MUSEUMS

Arc de Triomphe, 75008, metro Charles-de-Gaulle-Étoile (see map, p. 34), open every day.

Archaeological Crypt Notre-Dame, 1 place du Parvis, 75004, metro Cité (see map, p. 45), closed Mondays.

Arch de la Défense, metro Grande-Arche, open every day.

Bibliothèque nationale de France—François-Mitterrand, 11 quai François-Mauriac, 75013, metro Bibliothèque François-Mitterrand (see map, p. 5), closed Mondays.

Bibliotheque nationale de France—Richelieu, 58 rue de Richelieu, 75002, metro Bourse (see map, p. 21), closed Mondays.

Carnavalet Museum (history of Paris), 23 rue de Sévigné, 75004, metro St-Paul (see map, p. 53), open 10am–6pm, closed Mondays.

Catacombs, 75014, metro Denfert-Rochereau (see map, p. 4), closed Mondays.

Chapelle expiatoire, 29 rue Pasquier, 75008, metro St-Augustin (see map, p. 20), Thursdays, Fridays, and Saturday afternoons.

Cluny Museum of Medieval Art, 6 place Paul-Painlevé, 75005, metro Cluny-la-Sorbonne (see map, p. 79), closed Tuesdays.

Cognac–Jay Museum (18th century), 8 rue Elzevir, 75003, metro St-Paul (see map, p. 53), closed Mondays.

Conciergerie (Museum of the Revolution), 4 boulevard du Palais, 75001, metro Cité (see map, p. 44), open every day.

Dali Museum, 11 rue Poulbot, 75018, metro Abbesses (see map, p. 38), open 10am–6:30pm every day.

Delacroix Museum, 6 rue de Furstenberg, 75006, metro St-Germain-des-Prés (see map, p. 79), open 9:30am–5pm, closed Tuesdays.

Eiffel Tower, 75007, metro Champs-de-Mars (see map, p. 78), open 9:30am–11pm every day.

Eroticism (Museum of), 72 boulevard de Clichy, 75018, metro Blanche (see map, p. 35), open 10am–2pm every day.

Fakes (Museum of; Contrefaçon), 16 rue de la Faisanderie, 75016, metro Porte-Dauphine (see map, p. 34), closed Mondays.

Fashion Museum (Palais Galliera), 10 avenue Pierre-1er-de-Serbie, 75016, metro Iéna (see map, p. 34), closed Tuesdays, open for special exhibitions only.

Freemasonry Museum, 16 rue Cadet, 75009, metro Cadet or Grands-Boulevards (see map, p. 35), open 2–6pm, closed Sundays and Mondays.

Glasses and Lorgnettes Museum, 85 rue du Faubourg-St-Honoré, 75008, metro Concorde (see map, p. 35), open 10am–noon and 2–6pm Tuesday–Saturday.

Invalides (Military Museum), 75007, metro Invalides (see map, p. 78), open 10am–5pm, closed first Monday of every month.

Jacquemart-André (18th century and Renaissance, plus restaurant), 158 boulevard Haussmann, 75008, metro Miromesnil (see map, p. 34), open every day.

Jeu-de-Paume (contemporary art), 75001, metro Concorde, closed Mondays (see map, p. 20), temporary exhibitions only.

Le Corbusier (Villa La Roche), 8 square du Docteur-Blanche, 75016, metro Jasmin (see map, p. 4), closed Sundays and Monday morning.

Letters and Manuscripts Museum, 8 rue de Nesle, 75006, metro Odéon (see map, p. 44), open 10am–6pm, closed Monday–Wednesday.

Louvre Museum, 75001, metro Palais-Royal-Musée-du-Louvre (see map, p. 21), closed Tuesdays.

Maillol Museum, 61 rue de Grenelle, 75007, metro rue-du-Bac (see map, p. 79), closed Tuesdays.

Marmottan Museum (impressionists, especially Monet), 2 rue Louis-Boilly, 75018, metro La Muette (see map, p. 34), closed Mondays.

Money and the Paris Mint (La Monnaie), 11 quai Conti, 75006, metro Pont-Neuf (see map, p. 44), closed Mondays.

Montmartre Museum, 12 rue Cortot, 75018, metro Lamarck (see map, p. 38), closed Mondays.

Notre-Dame, Cathedral Towers, metro Cité (see map, p. 45), open 9:30am–7:30pm every day.

Orsay Museum, metro Solferino (see map, p. 20), closed Mondays.

Pantheon (Foucault's Pendulum), place du Panthéon, 75005, metro Maubert-Mutualité (see map, p. 79), open every day.

Paris Story **multimedia show,** 11 bis rue Scribe, 75009, metro Opéra (see map, p. 20), open every day, show every hour.

Playing Card Museum (Tarots), 16 rue Auguste-Gervais, 92130, Issy-les-Moulineaux, metro Mairie-d'Issy, closed Mondays and Tuesdays and Friday morning.

Police Museum, 4 rue de la Montagne-St-Genevieve, 75005, metro Maubert-Mutualité (see map, p. 79), open 9am–5pm, closed Sundays.

Pompidou Centre, 75004, metro Chatelet-les-Halles (see map, p. 53), closed Tuesdays.

Radio France Museum, 116 avenue du President-Kennedy, 75016, metro Ranelagh (see map, p. 34), closed Saturdays and Sundays, must reserve at tel. 01/56-40-15-16.

Sewers Museum (les Egouts), Left Bank end of Alma bridge, 75007, metro Alma-Marceau (see map, p. 78), closed Thursdays, Fridays, and the last three weeks of January.

Ste-Chapelle, 4 boulevard du Palais, 75001, metro Cité (see map, p. 44), open every day.

The Tower of John the Fearless, 20 rue Étienne-Marcel, 75002, metro Étienne-Marcel (see map, p. 21), open Wednesday, Saturday, and Sunday afternoons.

Victor Hugo Museum, 6 place des Vosges, 75004, metro St-Paul (see map, p. 53), closed Mondays, entrance free.

Religion Museums

Guimet Museum (Asiatic Art and Buddhism), 6 place d'Iéna, 75016, metro Iéna (see map, p. 34), closed Tuesdays.

Institute of the Arab World (pre- and post-Islamic culture), 1 rue des Fossés-St-Bernard, 75005, metro Jussieu (see map, p. 5).

Jewish Art and History Museum, 71 rue du Temple, 75003, metro Rambuteau (see map, p. 53), closed Saturdays.

Mosque of Paris, place du Puits-de-l'Hermite, 75005, metro Jussieu (see map, p. 79), closed Tuesdays.

Notre-Dame Museum, 10 rue du Cloître-Notre-Dame, 75004, metro Cité (see map, p. 45), open 2:30–6pm Wednesdays, Saturdays, and Sundays.

FOOD

Good food is available everywhere in Paris. Avoid the most touristy areas for anything other than a snack. The Champs-Élysées and Concorde areas tend to be especially expensive for food, coffee, and light meals. Look at the food already on people's plates to see if it looks like something that you may enjoy. If a restaurant is filled with locals and does not display an English menu outside, that is a good sign. A restaurant should always display a menu with prices outside the establishment. Ask for *la carte*. The English word *menu* means a fixed-priced menu with limited choice of starters, main course, and dessert. The *plat du jour*, or dish of the day, is usually fresh. The Latin Quarter, Montmartre, and the Marais have some of the best and most reasonable restaurants. A few restaurants are mentioned in this guide; however, they are included because of the appropriate and fun nature of their themes or décor rather than for the food. Good restaurant guides are available from the English bookshops recommended in this guide. The quality of restaurants changes quickly, so buy an up-to-date guide if you are keen on good food.

TIPPING AND CAFÉ ETIQUETTE

An astonishing number of guidebooks say not to tip in cafés and restaurants as service is included. Watch the locals and you'll see how wrong this is! Clients leave a few small coins in the change saucer after a quick coffee, a couple of euros after a lunch, and more after a restaurant meal. If you order at the bar, stay at the bar; if you wish to sit down, order from the table. Drinks are cheaper at the bar, which is why you should not take them to a table. Service is included, usually at 15 percent, but this is not a tip; it is the waiter's wage. Most waiters in cafés and brasseries get paid a small retaining wage, plus 15 percent of their daily takings. This charge is not included if you buy at the bar because the barman is effectively giving his service for free. If you have had nice service, leave a small gesture. Taxi drivers should also get to keep some change!

GETTING AROUND

TAKING THE METRO

The metro is the cheapest and easiest way to travel. A *carnet*

(CAR-nay) of 10 tickets is good value. You can buy weekly travel passes, but they run Monday–Sunday only. The day pass "Paris Visite" is worthwhile only if you are making more than the 10 *carnet* journeys. The *carnet* has no date limit and can be used on the bus, the metro, and the Montmartre funicular lift. Journeys on the RER (Réseau Express Régionale, the suburban train system) can have different tariffs if leaving zones 1, 2, or 3. Supplements are necessary for Versailles and the airports.

Taking a Cab

Cab drivers around the world have their own reputations. When traveling in a strange city it is easy to get the impression that a driver has taken you on a lengthy wild-goose chase. Most drivers have better things to do and no shortage of clients. If you are worried about this, then ask for a *fiche* as you get in. This is a receipt that records the starting and dropping points, price, and driver's reference. If you find that you can't flag a cab down, then you are probably within a couple of minutes' walk from a cab station.

Taking a Train

Train tickets can be bought at all railway stations, either at the *guichet* counter or by credit card from automatic distributors. There is an SNCF (French Rail) counter in the tourist office by the inverted pyramid in the Louvre, and there are usually very few people in line there; tickets are available for all over France and for Eurostar.

English Language Bookstores

The Red Wheelbarrow, 22 rue St-Paul, 75004, metro St-Paul (see map, p. 53).

Village Voice, 6 rue Princesse, 75006, metro Mabillon (around the corner from St-Sulpice, see map, p. 79).

San Francisco Bookstore, 17 rue Monsieur-le-Prince, 75006, metro Mabillon or Odéon (see map, p. 79).

Tea and Tattered Pages, 24 rue Mayet, 75006, metro Duroc (see map, p. 78).

APPENDIX 1:
THE
SEVEN
SEALS

ARS MAGNA

DAN BROWN is passionate about anagrams. He tells us that the mystical teachings of the Cabala drew heavily on these, and that the French monarchs believed in their magical power. The Romans, he tells us convincingly, referred to this study as Ars Magna, or "the Great Art." This is not true, but typical of Brown's brilliance, Ars Magna is simply an anagram of "anagrams"! Word games in general appear throughout the book, so keep your eyes constantly open as you read. Brown's *Angels and Demons* employs another word game called Ambigrams; these are words that read the same both right-side up and upside down.

Langdon's Dictionary of Symbols, Sacred and Profane

Let him that hath understanding count the number of the Beast: for it is the number of a man; and his number is 666."

—Book of Revelations 13:18

This section looks at some of the main issues raised in *The Da Vinci Code*, especially the power of symbols. The name "Seven Seals" comes from the last book of the Bible, the Apocalypse or Revelation of John the Divine. The word "apocalypse" comes from the Greek and means "unveiling." This book is a fantastic allegory, evoking strange creatures such as a seven-headed monster, plagues of giant locusts, and a lamb with seven eyes and 10 horns. It is "a coherent symbolic set," as Langdon the Harvard symbologist would call it. At the beginning of the book, seven seals are broken, and as each seal is unlocked, the messages in John's vision are revealed.

The book of Revelation is an important source of symbols for religious artists, particularly during the early medieval period. Dan Brown's use of the symbols from this book includes the number 666. Symbols are strangely powerful, capable of conveying a strong message. The "Ban the Bomb" sign of the 1960s evokes peace while a skull and crossbones carries a message of danger.

As with all symbols, the Apocalypse has been adopted and interpreted differently through succeeding ages. The book was written at the end of the 1st century AD and refers to the contemporary conditions of Christians under the Roman Empire. The vision described and its symbols were a thinly disguised or coded criticism of non-Christian powers, especially those of Rome, symbolized by the "Whore of Babylon." The figure of the Beast stood for pagan Emperor Nero, but its meaning changed through time. Later it came to signify Islam to the crusading Christians, Protestant heresy to the Catholics during the Reformation, and for the Lutherans, it symbolized the corrupt papacy.

The fantastic images from the Revelation, the symbolism of which is often obscure, can be seen in medieval manuscripts, stained-glass windows, frescoes, engravings, and tapestries. The best example of this in Paris is the rose window of the Ste-Chapelle, dating from the end of the 15th century. The story is told from the center of the window outward, each concentric ring of glass showing the events that take place as each of the seven seals is broken and the book is opened to reveal what lies within.

COMMON SYMBOLS IN ART THROUGHOUT THE AGES

666. When Langdon explains the pentagram to Fache, he also explains that the difficulty in deciphering a symbol comes from the fact that it is different for all people. The pentacle in modern culture has become associated with devil worship and used as a satanic symbol in horror movies. The same has happened to the number 666.

Dan Brown tells us that 666 is the number of panes of glass in Mitterrand's pyramid. Originally this number appears in the Revelation of John the Divine 13:18, and the verse says it is "the number of the Beast." This is actually an allusion to Emperor Nero. The study of numeric values in words is known as *gematria*. When analyzed in this manner, the name Caesar Neron in Greek equals 666. Greek is used because it is the language of the original book of Revelation. Three consecutive rolls of a dice resulting in 666 are considered to be unlucky; this is often erroneously said to come from the Great Fire of London, although it did take place in 1666. Dan Brown writes that the book of meditations used by Opus Dei consists of 999 maxims. (Presumably members are told to keep the book the right way up.)

In biblical numerology, seven equals perfection, and there are seven days for creation and seven days of the week. Six equals imperfection, and 666, being threefold, forms a trinity of imperfection. When analyzed in the same way, the name of Jesus in Greek equals 888, and this is interpreted as the number of superperfection.

Ankh. A cross topped with a loop, the ankh appears frequently in Egyptian art. Its original meaning is still debated but its hieroglyphic meaning is "life." For this reason

it is a frequent attribute of the gods and is often shown being handed to the king. As a symbol it points to divine and eternal life. The ankh was adopted by the Coptic Church (the Christian church in Egypt) and called the Crux Ansata. Saunière has added a collection of ankhs to the Louvre because of the ankh's association with the goddess and life-giving attributes. (☞ *See the* Under the Pyramids *chapter.*)

Apples. A very important symbol in *The Da Vinci Code*, the word "apple" opens the final Cryptex. In Christian images the apple is the fruit of the tree of knowledge and symbolizes the fall of Eve. This symbol descends fom Greek mythology. The daughters of Atlas guarded the golden fruit of an apple tree with the help of a snake, but Hercules stole the apples. In mythology, Paris, the Trojan prince, awards a golden apple to Venus. This gift causes the Trojan war. Apples are also the attributes of the three graces, the handmaidens of Venus. (☞ *See* Venus de Milo *in the* Under the Pyramids *chapter.*) When shown held by the infant Christ, the fruit symbolizes his role as Redeemer.

Baphomet. This figure is really the key to *The Da Vinci Code*. Baphomet is represented as a human figure with wings and horns, like a rebel angel. Under torture, the Templars admitted to worshiping him. The biblical scholar Hugh Schonfield applied the Atbash Cipher to the name and found that once decoded, it revealed  the word "Sophia," which means "wisdom" in Greek. Sophia is also the goddess considered to be the bride of God. (☞ *See the* Sacred Tetragrammaton *in the* Beneath the Rose Line *chapter.*) From this it is argued that the Templars were worshipers and protectors of the sacred feminine. A sculpture of Baphomet can be seen crowning the portal of the Church of St-Merry.

Blade and Chalice. The two symbols (Λ V) represent respectively the phallus or male and the womb or the feminine. They are alluded to throughout *The Da Vinci Code*. One placed above the other makes a sacred union of male and female and forms the hourglass shape of the Holy Grail. The Grail itself symbolizes union, the womb, and the bloodline. Superimposed on top of each other blade and chalice make a star of David. This is also the shape of I. M. Pei's inverted pyramid complex at the Louvre, a fact exploited to wonderful effect by Dan Brown.

Caduceus. This is the staff of Mercury. It is intertwined with two snakes and topped with wings. The staff was used by Mercury to separate two fighting serpents and therefore symbolizes peace. The symbol is used by the medical and business world. This is because of an ancient belief in the healing powers of snake venom and because of the fact that peace is always good for business. There is also a link between the words "mercantile/merchants" and the name Mercury.

Chi-Rho. This monogram can be seen in most churches and consists of the Greek letters chi and rho, the first two letters of Christ's name. It is commonly found in Christian art from the 4th century, often between the symbols A and W, alpha and omega. It was originally used in pre-Christian times, when it was a symbol of good omen (the letters are an abbreviation of the Greek word *chrestos*, meaning "auspicious"). The symbol was adopted by Emperor Constantine for the Imperial Roman standard, probably for pagan rather than Christian reasons. This sign appeared in a dream to Constantine before his battle with Maxentius.

Fish. A symbol of both Christ and baptism. The Greek word for fish, ΙΧΘΥΣ, forms the initials of Jesus/Christ/of God/the Son/Savior. In the 1st and 2nd centuries, believers were called *pisciculi*, or "little fishes," and the baptismal font *piscina*, literally "fish pond." The font is often octagonal or eight-sided—seven is the number of man, one the number of God, and the total of eight equals perfection.

Fleur-de-Lis. The white lily symbolizes purity, and it has been used by the French monarchs since the 12th century. The fleur-de-lis, formed like the pointed end of a lance, also represents military force. The lily as a symbol of purity frequently appears in paintings of the Annunciation.

Greek Cross. Cross with four arms of equal length.

Holy Grail. According to legend, it is the vessel used by Jesus at the Last Supper and later by Joseph of Arimathea to collect and preserve the blood of Christ after the Crucifixion. The miraculous vessel predates Christianity and is a feminine symbol representing the womb in which life-giving transformation occurs. The vessel or vase was central to alchemical tradition in ancient China and this reached Northern Europe in the 12th century. Medieval mystics saw it as a representation of the soul, to be filled and replenished with divine grace. *The Da Vinci Code* theory that the Grail is the relics of Mary Magdalene, giver of life, is based upon this interpretation. In the book, the Grail consists of an actual tomb, physical relics, and documents relating to Mary Magdalene. Saint Graal means "Holy Cup" or "Chalice," but it is also interpreted as "Sang Real" or "Royal Blood."

IHS. Abbreviation of the name Jesus in Latin.

INRI. Latin inscription pinned on the cross at the Crucifixion, written by Pilate to mock Christ: Iesus Nazarenus Rex Iudaeorum—Jesus of Nazareth, King of the Jews. These initials are often shown on the cross in paintings or sculptures of the Crucifixion.

Lamb. Symbol of sacrifice. (☞ *For a full explanation see* Tempus Fugit *in the* Beneath the Rose Line *chapter.*)

Olympic Rings. Langdon attributes esoteric origins to

the Olympic rings, linking them to the eight-year cycle of the planet Venus, around which the original games were organized. According to the Olympic Charter, the five rings were chosen by Pierre de Coubertin in 1913 to symbolize the union of five continents. The games are held every four years, and this period is called an Olympiad. The first Olympic games in Paris were in 1900, the second in 1924.

Pelican. A myth said that the pelican would pluck flesh from her own breast to feed her young. This led to the bird's becoming a symbol of sacrifice and therefore of the Crucifixion. A beautifully sculpted example of this can be seen on the roof of the sacristy at the back end of St-Sulpice Church.

Pentacle. An ancient pagan symbol in the form of a five-pointed star. Langdon says it is associated with devil worship, but it actually represents the sacred feminine or divine goddess. It is a symbol of Venus because the planet supposedly traces a pentacle in the sky. The pentacle symbolizes perfection and beauty because the sections it creates correspond to the Golden Mean. In Christian iconography it has been used to symbolize the five wounds of Christ. For Pythagoras, the pentacle was the symbol of man, encompassing the five points (head and limbs) of the Vitruvian Man. It also corresponds to the five elements from which man was believed to be made up: earth, water, fire, air, and psyche, or plasma.

Rose. Teabing says the rose is the Priory symbol for the Grail, which is in effect Mary Magdalene. It is linked to the pentacle by its five-petaled form, and it is also the anagram of Eros, god of sexual love. The rose was brought back from the Holy Lands by the Crusaders and became a sign of romantic love; it was adopted by the neo-Platonists and evolved first as a symbol of pure love and then as a symbol of the Virgin Mary. The rose windows on cathedrals dedicated to Notre Dame are symbols of this. The Virgin Mary can be seen standing in front of the central rose on the west façade of Notre-Dame in Paris. The rose was sacred to Venus in antiquity and is her attribute in Renaissance and later art, at which time the pricking of its thorns was associated with the wounds of love.

Snake. The Red Snake of the *Dossiers Secrets* symbolizes the bloodline of Christ. In Christian iconography the serpent represents evil or Satan, but for the ancients the snake symbolized fertility, wisdom, and the power to heal. In the Lady Chapel at St-Sulpice, the Virgin, sculpted by Jean-Baptiste Pigalle, is treading on the serpent, symbolizing the vanquishing of sin. The snake is also the symbol of prudence. ("Be wary as serpents." Matthew 10:16)

Swastika. Perhaps no better example exists of the power of symbols. The swastika is extremely ancient. It can be drawn both left- and right-facing. This symbol had universally positive connotations until the rise of Fascism. It was used by Hindus to symbolize universal stability. In Buddhism it is called *manji* and represents universal harmony. In Jaïnism it is an auspicious symbol. Until the rise of Fascism, Rudyard Kipling incorporated a swastika in his book covers, symbolizing his interest in Indian culture. Many companies used this emblem as a logo: the Finnish air force and army, the Swedish company AESA, even the Boy Scouts in Britain. Once adopted by Nazi Germany, the symbol became synonymous with terror. This corruption of an ancient and powerful symbol has led to its becoming taboo in modern times.

How Symbols Change Through Time

Star of David or Solomon's Seal. Two interlocking triangles, these are the blade and chalice once again. The six-pointed star is recognized today as the universal symbol of

the Jewish people. The symbol is, however, extremely ancient and was used by occult groups before taking on its modern symbolism. Some Orthodox Jewish groups reject its use because of its association with magic and the occult. It is an important astrological symbol in Zoroastrianism. The first mention of it in rabbinic literature is in the mid-12th century. Jewish lore suggests that either King David had this emblem on his shield or that his shield was this shape, and it is thus a symbol of protection. Proof of the power of symbols as described by Langdon, and particularly of their adoption and shifting meaning, is the yellow star that Jews were made to wear during the Holocaust. This was extended to all Jews older than the age of six in German-occupied areas on September 6, 1941. Triangular badges that were color-coded were forced upon other groups too. The Nazis obliged homosexuals to wear a pink triangle. This illustrates the organic nature of the symbol. The pink triangle is today internationally recognized as identifying the gay community. Various badges are exhibited at the beautiful and poignant Monument to the Deported.

☞ *The Monument to the Deported is in the square de l'Île-de-France, behind Notre-Dame (see map, p. 45).*
☞ *See also the synagogue by Hector Guimard, rue Pavé (see map, p. 53), and the Renaissance chapel of the École des Beaux-Arts, rue Bonaparte, 75006 (see map, p. 21).*

An Alchemical Distillation of Main Issues Raised in *The Da Vinci Code*

Many books that have been written about *The Da Vinci Code* violently attack its content and debunk the theories developed. These have mostly been written by Christian groups or authors. This has the adverse affect of adding fuel to the fire as it reinforces the idea that there really is something to hide.

However, many of the main issues raised by Dan Brown have caused contention. The theories upheld by his heroes are based on a wide range of research. The following books develop the main issues in depth. If you wish to do some further reading, these are good places to start.

Holy Blood, Holy Grail. Michael Baigent, Richard Leigh, and Henry Lincoln. Arrow Books, 1982.

The Templar Revelation: Secret Guardians of the True Identity of Christ. Lynn Picknett and Clive Prince. Touchstone, 1998.

The Woman with the Alabaster Jar: Mary Magdalen and the Holy Grail. Margaret Starbird. Bear and Company, 1993.

The Passover Plot. Hugh Schonfield. Element Books, reissue 1998.

The Code Book: The Science of Secrecy from Ancient Egypt to Quantum Cryptography. Simon Singh. Anchor Books, 1999.

A GREAT TREASURE

Somewhere in Europe a great treasure is hidden. Its exact content is not known, nor are the identities of those who hid it or keep it hidden. The temple in Jerusalem was sacked by the Romans in 70 AD and the contents of the Holy of Holies was taken back to Rome. This treasure may have included the Ark of the Covenant. The great treasure may also have been that of the Merovingian kings, or that of Margaret of Provence. She carried a fortune with her to pay the ransom wanted for her husband, St-Louis, but on learning of his death, she is said to have hidden it.

The Cathars were also purported to have kept something of extraordinary value that was probably sacred. This could have been hidden or passed onto the Templars at the time of the Albigensian Crusades, as many high-ranking Templars were of Cathar families. Later on the Freemasons appropriated the Templars as their antecedents and may have become guardians of the treasure. Sion is the symbol of the temple, and it is argued that the Priory of Sion became the keepers of the secret. The question asked is whether this could be the treasure that the real-life Saunière found at Rennes-le-Château?

Wedding Vows

It is argued that the above-mentioned treasure is more than wealth, rather that it is a sacred symbol of the marriage of Christ and Mary Magdalene—a symbol that could prove that the divinity of Christ was invented by man and that Christ fathered a line of descendants who became the Merovingians. The association of Mary Magdalene with France is alluded to in the account of her life in *The Golden Legend*. What are believed to be her relics, including a skull, are kept at the Basilique St-Marie-Madeleine at St-Maximin in Provence.

Some of the main arguments put forward to support the theory of Christ's marriage come from the New Testament, others from the Gnostic Gospels. It is said that it would have been very unusual for Christ not to be married and that if he were not, it would have been mentioned in the Bible. Mary Magdalene anoints Christ with spikenard. This is an ointment that was used at wedding ceremonies, and it was apparently used by Mary Magdalene to anoint Christ at the wedding of Cana. It is said that this event probably represents their own marriage. Jesus did not preach celibacy (Matthew 19:4–5).

Mary Magdalene is with Christ at the most crucial moments of his life, including the Crucifixion and his burial. She is the first to see him after the Resurrection.

Other arguments are:

Jesus treated women as equals, but later writers of the epistles contributed to the suppression of the role of women. In the Nag Hammadi text known as the Gospel of Mary, we learn of Andrew's disbelief concerning Mary Magdalene's seeing Christ resurrected, and we read of Peter's jealousy over Mary Magdalene.

Jesus treats women in an extraordinary way. For example, he ignores the ritual impurity laws in Mark 5:25–34 and refers to women as "daughters of Abraham" in Luke

13:16. In Luke 7:35 Jesus refers to both women and men as children of wisdom and in Luke 8:1–3 he demonstrates that women were part of his inner circle. He talked to foreign women in John 4:7, and he taught women in Luke 10:38–42, when he teaches Martha, for example. These are just a few of the arguments put forward in the above books. (☞ *For more information, read the* Isis and the Sacred Feminine *appendix*).

GNOSTICS

Dan Brown evokes the Gnostics. Little was known about Gnosticism until the discovery of the Nag Hammadi texts in the mid-20th century. This system of religious belief was prominent by the 2nd century AD but was seen as heretical by the early church. One of the Gnostic Gospels most often referred to is the Gospel of Thomas, which describes Christ and Sophia as aspects of God that make up the complete God, known as the Pleroma. Another important text is known as the Pistis Sophia, which links Sophia to Mary Magdalene, and there is a Gnostic Gospel of Mary that proclaims the preeminence of Mary Magdalene, whom the Gnostics are believed to have venerated in the form of the sacred feminine. The Cathars and the Templars are said to have maintained this tradition, becoming the guardians of her sacred relics.

A BARROW FULL OF BOOKS

Abigail and Penelope run the well-stocked English-language bookstore The Red Wheel Barrow. You can buy or order the previously listed book titles from them. Penelope and Abigail's names are decoded for you. You can ask them to decode the name of their shop.

Abigail. A Hebrew name meaning "a father's joy." In the first book of Samuel, Abigail is "a woman of good understanding and of a beautiful countenance." In the play *The Scornful Lady,* by William Shakespeare's contemporaries Francis Beaumont and John Fletcher, Abigail is the heroine's confidential helper. As a result, Abigail came to mean any confidential attendant. After the Reformation many Old Testament names became popular in England.

Penelope. The wife of Ulysses, ruler of Ithaca. While Ulysses was absent fighting the Trojan wars, Penelope had many suitors, who tried to convince her that her husband would never return. To delay the suitors Penelope agreed that she would make her choice once the cloth she was weaving was finished. Each night she unraveled her work and began again. The suitors took up residence in her home and held riotous parties, but when Ulysses returned, he slew them, and with Penelope, once again ruled over Ithaca. The name became widespread in the 17th century. According to old Welsh tales Penelope is a "fairy name."

The shop is at 22 rue St-Paul in the heart of the old Marais Quarter near metro St-Paul (see map, p. 53).

APPENDIX 2:
INSIDE
THE
CRYPTEX

THE CRYPTEX is a design of genius. Historically it does not appear to have actually existed although the ancients had many ingenious ways to protect secrets, including both the use of codes and lockable devices. As early as the 5th century BC, the Greeks used a form of Cryptex called the Spartan Scytale. It consisted of a message written on a long band, which could be read only if it were wound around the correct-size baton, allowing the letters to align into a coherent text. One of the recent books written about *The Da Vinci Code* criticizes Brown by arguing that there is no way the Cryptex would work, saying that the vinegar in the internal phial could not possibly dissolve papyrus. This may be true, but it is likely that the vinegar would make a terrible mess of the ink! There seems to be no evidence that da Vinci invented the device; it seems to be a true creation of Brown's. The concept and the name are brilliant. Cryptex appears in no dictionary (yet!) and is therefore a neologism, very probably of Brown's own invention. Now the conundrum: If it does not really exist, how come there is a photo? It seems that the real Leonardo behind the Cryptex is Justin Nevins. You can see, and even order, his beautiful work at www.cryptex.org. He hand-makes these objects according to his own design and his customer's specifications. In a recent interview I asked him how he acquired the secret. He replied that it had been handed down to him by a grand master of the Priory of Sion! Each one takes him 4–6 weeks to make, and it can be made from a variety of different materials, including metal, stone, and beautiful wood. Justin has been fascinated by games and puzzles since he was a child, and creating the Cryptex was obviously an irresistible challenge for him. So far he has made about 100. His favorites are not necessarily the ones that use the most precious materials, but the ones that incorporate his client's most ingenious and personal clues. Set yourself the challenge, work out your code, and order your Cryptex!

Sophie's World:
The *Who's Who* of *The Da Vinci Code*

D an Brown has presented his readers a cast of colorful characters that some literary critics have called shallow and trite. A careful look at their character traits, every personal detail, and their names reveals the Joycean web woven by Brown. The description of each character is completed with suggestions of what he or she might have done in Paris.

SANDRINE BIEIL

Here we find two names linked with the quest for the Holy Grail. The Abbé Bieil was the director general of the Seminary of St-Sulpice when the real-life Saunière of Rennes-le-Château brought the mysterious documents he discovered to the church. Gino Sandri, from whom Brown takes the name Sandrine, was the personal secretary of Pierre Plantard, the grand master of the Priory of Sion in modern times. The nun, guardian of the keystone, is murdered in the church by Silas.

☞ *Living in the church she would have done her shopping at the lovely nearby covered market—the Marché St-Germain, 75006, metro Odéon or Mabillon—with its food shops, boutiques, and restaurants.*

☞ *She also probably bought homemade produce (jams, biscuits, incense, essential oils) from the monastery shop of Paris, Monastic Produce, boutique of the Fraternité monastique de Jérusalem, 10 rue des Barres, 75004, metro Hôtel-de-Ville (see map, p. 53).*

☞ *Shops specializing in devotional objects are all around St-Sulpice (see map, p. 79), especially rue du Vieux-Colombier.*

BISHOP ARINGAROSA

The Opus Dei cardinal is devoted to saving his church by obtaining the Grail before anyone else. He is well meaning but has been duped. He is mortified at the deaths caused by his efforts and ever-forgiving. He is the patron of Silas, as Frollot is the patron of Quasimodo in another thriller set in Paris. At first we are led to believe he is the villain, but his Italian name *aringa* and *rosa* means "red herring." There is a hidden rose in his name, and his Christian name Manuel means "guide" or "handbook."

☞ *Aringarosa's favorites would include the Shrine of St-Vincent de Paul. This saint was associated with the Compagnie du St-Sacrement at St-Sulpice. The saint's body is preserved in a spectacular glass reliquary case and can be seen at the chapelle des prêtres de la Mission lazariste, 95 rue de Sèvres, 75006, metro Vaneau (see map, p. 78).*

☞ *He would also worship at the Church of the Miraculous Medal, rue du Bac, 75007, metro Sèvres-Babylone (see map, p. 79).*

☞ *The extraordinary tomb of Richelieu in the chapel of the Sorbonne, place de la Sorbonne, 75005, metro Cluny (see map, p. 79), would fascinate him. Richelieu is shown in the act of dropping dead, supported by two muses, with his enormous cardinal's hat hovering above the sepulchre.*

La Sorbonne

JÉROME COLLET

The assistant to Fache follows the trail through the book but always seems to be one step behind, although his name in French means "a noose" or "to snare." Collet is made to feel rather uncomfortable, alone at night in Saunière's office, being stared at by the meter-tall model knight in armor.

☞ *A cure for his phobia could be a visit to the armor galleries at the superb Military Museum, les Invalides, 75007 (which includes Napoleon's Tomb), metro Invalides (see map, p. 78), open 10am–5pm every day except the first Monday of the month.*

(Captain) Bezu Fache

He carries himself like an angry ox and is therefore Le Taureau (the bull). Fache is deeply religious and later shows great compassion to Aringarosa. He is described in chapter 4 as having "hair slicked back with oil ... an arrow-like widow's peak that ... preceded him like the prow of a battleship." The arrow is the sign of the male, and the prow of a ship is the symbol of Paris. Fache evokes the French word for "anger," and Bezu is a mysterious mountain close to Rennes-le-Château, associated with the Templars. The captain is part of the Direction centrale de police judiciaire (DCPJ), which is an equivalent of the FBI.

☞ *Fache's favorites would include the Police Museum, 4 rue de la Montagne-St-Geneviève, 75005, metro Maubert-Mutualité (see map, p. 79), open 9am–5pm, closed Sundays (free), a wonderful collection of documents and objects that evoke famous crimes and mysteries, including the blade of the guillotine used in the Revolution.*

Jonas Faukman

Another subtle anagram—Jason Kaufman is Dan Brown's real editor. Jonas plays a minor, but key, role and has the most telling line in the book. It is he who sent Langdon's book to Saunière for approval, setting in motion the "Langdon-commits-murder" connection. When Langdon presents his manuscript, *Symbols of the Lost Sacred Feminine*, to his publisher, Faukman says, "You're a Harvard historian, for God's sake, not a pop schlockmeister looking for a quick buck." Is this Brown's conscience speaking? Apparently Kaufman negotiated a two-book deal for Brown worth half a million dollars.

☞ *In Paris, any editor would stroll along the rue Servandoni (see map, p. 79) and make a pilgrimage to one of Paris's most literary streets, rue de l'Odéon (see map, p. 79), and admire the windows of the city's editors, ancient bookshops, and charming Old World bookbinders. This is where Sylvia Beach had her famous bookshop Shakespeare and Company. The world of editors has been in the Latin Quarter since the Sorbonne obtained its first printing press in late medieval times.*

Claude Grouard

Grouard is the security warden at the Louvre, forced to release Sophie and Langdon when she takes a painting hostage. He was very fond of his boss Saunière. He's an adoring security agent whose name is an anagram of ardor and cudgel! Favorites in Paris: days when the Louvre is on strike!

ROBERT LANGDON

Harvard symbologist (the expression does not exist but will undoubtedly enter the English language soon). Real-life John Langdon seemingly invented the Ambigram, which is a word that reads the same upside down or the right way up. Some examples can be seen at www.johnlangdon.net. A Scots gardener called Charles Jencks has created a garden around this theme. Langdon is past middle age, brilliant, attractive, and a specialist in the symbols of the sacred feminine. "Lang" is like language, and "don" is a university lecturer. His name makes the anagram "Art golden born."

☞ *Langdon's favorites would be the National Archives Museum, 87 rue Vieille-du-Temple (see map, p. 53), and Cabinet of Antiquities, Bibliothèque Nationale, 58 rue de Richelieu, 75002, metro Bourse or Pyramides (free, see map, p. 21).*

☞ *He would also enjoy the Bibliothèque Nationale de France—François-Mitterrand, 11 quai François-Mauriac, 75013, metro Bibliothèque François-Mitterrand (see map, p. 5). Its fantastic modern architecture includes four towers symbolizing open books around a sunken pine forest.*

☞ *Having experienced being trapped in a Dali painting, he'd try the Dali Museum, 11 rue Poulbot, 75018, metro Abbesses (see map, p. 38), open 10am–6:30pm every day.*

RÉMY LEGALUDEC

Rémy is the cool but overly ambitious manservant of Teabing. He does all the Teacher's dirty work and is then killed off, thanks to the Teacher's knowledge of his allergy to nuts. He attempts to save the day several times but is mercilessly murdered. His name is an anagram of his two functions in the story: a cudgel and allergy. There is a beautiful park in the 13th arrondisement called square René-Le Gall, the trees of which follow the banks of the ancient Bievre River. In among the obelisks and pergolas, it is perfect for a picnic. Next door is the maternity clinic, the Villa Isis. The Observatory of Paris, the starting point of the Rose Line, can be seen at nearby metro Port-Royal.

☞ *Legaludec's bugging skills would have led him to the Radio France Museum, 116 avenue du Président-Kennedy, 75016, metro Ranelagh (see map, p. 34), closed weekends, must reserve at tel. 01/56-40-15-16.*

BÉRENGER SAUNIÈRE

This nonfictional character was the poor parish priest at the heart of the Grail mystery evoked in the book *Holy Blood, Holy Grail,* by Michael Baigent, Richard Leigh, and Henry Lincoln. His life story is a tangle of confusing leads that has caused furor among researchers and is the catalyst for *The Da Vinci Code.* His sudden and extravagant spending aroused the suspicions of local ecclesiastics. He was accused of illicitly selling Masses and was suspended from his post. Saunière appealed to the Vatican, his suspension was over-ruled, and he was reinstated. (He was obviously a man of great influence.) He died on January 17, 1917, the feast day of St-Sulpice. January 17 is also inscribed on one of the tombstones in his churchyard. The inscription on the same tombstone was a coded message containing references to Nicolas Poussin and Teniers as a key to the same message that Saunière found hidden in his church. He had the tombstone inscription removed, not knowing it had previously been copied. (☞ *To further your quest, see* Nicolas Poussin in the Under the Pyramids *chapter.*)

☞ *Saunière's favorites would include an extravagant shopping spree at Galeries Lafayette and Printemps, department stores behind the Opera, metro Havre-Caumartin (see map, p. 20), and who knows, perhaps the Museum of Fakes, the Contrefaçon, 16 rue de la Faisanderie, 75016, metro Porte Dauphine (see map, p. 34).*

JACQUES SAUNIÈRE

Saunière takes his family name from the priest at Rennes-le-Château and his Christian name from Jacques de Molay. In the book he is curator of the Louvre, grand master of the Priory of Sion, grandfather of Sophie Neveu, specialist of goddess symbols, and guardian of the Grail—a busy man who still found time to practice Hieros Gamos! (☞ *Look in the* Under the Pyramids *chapter to rediscover the incredible message he has time to leave before expiring in the Louvre.*)

☞ *As Jacques is dead, go visit the Cemetery of Père-Lachaise, metro Père-Lachaise (see map, p. 5). Tombs of the famous and infamous, beautiful and macabre. Open every day. Look out for the tomb of Allan Kardec, founder of spiritism. It is a copy of a prehistoric pagan burial monument and one of the most visited tombs in this graveyard.*

SILAS

He's a "hulking albino" who, like Quasimodo, was adopted by a church superior. His loyalty to Opus Dei pushed him to commit a pentacle of five murders. His name is that of a Bible character whose story is told in Acts 15 and 16, notably in 16:26. He is one of Paul's main missionary companions. Biblical Silas is released from prison with Paul after an earthquake destroys the building. In Acts 15:41 he "confirms the churches of Cilicia." His own name evokes both Cilicia and the *cilice* belt that he wears.

☞ *Visit rue La Bruyère in the 9th arrondisement (see map, p. 35) to look for the house where Silas takes a much-needed rest after murdering Sandrine Bieil.*

☞ *Can't find Opus Dei? Then visit the nearby Gustave Moreau Museum, 14 rue de La Rochefoucauld, 75009, metro Trinité (see map, p. 35), open 10am–noon, 2–5pm, closed Tuesdays, to see mysterious symbolist paintings or the Museum of Romantic Life, 16 rue Chaptal, 75009, metro Trinité (see map, p. 35), open 10am–6pm, closed Mondays, for souvenirs of George Sand, Frédéric Chopin, and 19th-century bohemian life.*

SOPHIE NEVEU

This is a name containing appropriate clues, including the initials of the Priory of Sion. Neveu is close to the French word for "new" and Eve can be found in her name. Is she the new Eve? Her name can be made into anagram of "Oh, Supine Eve." This would evoke the fallen woman having been forced to become submissive. In Greek, Sofia means "wisdom" and also contains the syllable phi, the name of the Golden Section. The Gnostics consider Sofia as the mystical consort of Christ. This belief is based on a Nag Hammadi text known as Sofia (Wisdom) of Christ. Is Sophie Neveu herself a Grail, carrying the bloodline of Christ? Dan Brown hints at this but chooses not to resolve the question. The name is sheer cryptic brilliance (hats off to Dan Brown). The French version of "Friends reunited" website, "Copains d'avant," has registered 10,081 Neveus in France but surprisingly not one Bézu!

☞ *Sophie is an attractive but unusually unfashionable Parisian, in sweater, leggings, and hair that "fell unstyled to her shoulders." She probably does her shopping at the wonderful flea market at Porte de Clignancourt (see map, p. 5). Why not invite her to Paris's Fashion Museum, Palais Galliera, avenue Pierre-1er-de-Serbie, 75016, metro Iéna (see map, p. 34)? The Flame of Liberty, which stands nearby at Alma Bridge (see map, p. 78), has become the unofficial monument to a modern female idol, Lady Diana.*

LEIGH TEABING

Here's a man of knowledge who could teach us a thing or two! Leigh Teabing, what a hodgepodge. Quintessential English gent, hence the Tea. Teabing is an anagram of one of the authors of *Holy Blood, Holy Grail*, and Leigh is the second author's name. The third contributor, Lincoln, is alluded to in the life of Teabing, notably in his role of making TV programs. At first he is presented as a charming rascal and then he is shown as a villain. Could this be a reflection of Brown's opinion of their book? Teabing is also exceedingly rich. I'm still perplexed by the leg irons (please send any suggestions to bartillat@wanadoo.fr).

☞ *Teabing could be found ambling through the lovely old covered arcades of Paris, like passage des Panoramas, passage Jouffroy, and passage Verdeau, 75002 and 75009, metro Grands-Boulevards (see map, p. 21), looking for ancient papers, documents, parchments, and statuettes for his mantelpiece.*

☞ *His favorite boutique is probably the tiny shop specializing in collectible walking sticks, just inside passage Jouffroy, M. G. Segas, 34 passage Jouffroy, 75009 (see map, p. 21).*

☞ *He would also like the Letters and Manuscripts Museum, 8 rue de Nesle, 75006, metro Odéon (see map, p. 44), open*

10am–6pm Thursday–Sunday, and Louvre des Antiquaires, place du Palais-Royal, 75001.

☞ Also, Angelina's, a famous tearoom with beautiful pâtisseries, although you won't find the scones that Teabing serves his late-night visitors (see map, p. 20).

PAMELA GETTUM

Irresistible Pamela! Welcoming, warm, smiling, and efficient. The name Pamela is another of Brown's sharp Greek references. It was coined by Philip Sidney in the 1580s in his romance *Arcadia* (is this a reference to Poussin again?). Sidney combined "pan," meaning "all," with "meli," meaning "honey"; our librarian is certainly all honey. The imagery in her chapter (92) is almost Shakespearean: Eyes are everywhere, perfect for a library. Pamela wears thick horn-rimmed glasses, she winks twice in three sentences, she eyes bits of paper, she shoots quick glances, and she also makes tea for weary researchers. As for Gettum, need I say more?

☞ Her favorites in Paris—the English-language bookstores (see p. 157 for map references): The Red Wheelbarrow, 22 rue St-Paul, 75004, metro St-Paul; Village Voice, 6 rue Princesse, 75006, metro Mabillon (around the corner from St-Sulpice); San Francisco Bookstore, 17 rue Monsieur-le-Prince, 75006, metro Mabillon or Odéon; Tea and Tattered Pages, 24 rue Mayet, 75006, metro Duroc.

☞ And of course she would like the Glasses and Lorgnettes Museum, 85 rue du Faubourg-St-Honoré, 75008, metro Concorde (see map, p. 35), open 10am–noon and 2–6pm Tuesday–Saturday.

ANDRÉ VERNET

André Vernet is the manager of the Depository Bank of Zurich and therefore indirectly the protector of the keystone. He is an old friend of Saunière and of course his initials A and V symbolize blade and chalice! Dan Brown doesn't miss a chance. The name also appears in the many acknowledgments Brown makes in his book. As he is the protector of a great treasure, he is perhaps Brown's contented bank manager?

☞ His favorite in Paris would be the Paris Mint (La Monnaie), 11 quai Conti, 75006, metro Pont-Neuf (see map, p. 44), for its history of money, fabrication of coins and medals, and collection of coins through the ages.

The Da Vinci Code Glossary

Alchemist/Alchemy. ( *See the* House of Nicolas Flamel *under* Sophie and Langdon's Right Bank *in the* Paving Stones of Paris *chapter and* Philosopher's Stone *in this Glossary.*)

Amon. An Egyptian god, his name means "the hidden one"; he was thought of as the power behind the sun. His headdress consists of a sun disk and feathers symbolizing truth. He is a god of fertility. Therefore, his symbols are the ram's horns and the snake. The spiral amonite shell is named after Amon's spiraling horns.

Apocrypha. Greek word meaning "hidden things." This expression was originally applied to any writing restricted to members of a secret society or sect. Among Christians it was applied to texts not included in the Bible. There are two categories of apocrypha: the books not found in the Hebrew Old Testament but included in the Septuagint (the pre-Christian Greek translation of the Hebrew), and the 40 or so books relating to Old and New Testament characters who have been denied scriptural authority and don't appear in the Christian Bible. Many Christian images are drawn from these books. (*See the story of Heliodorus under* A Repentant Sinner *in the Delacroix section of St-Sulpice in the* Under the Rose Line *chapter.*)

Arago Plaques. These medallions give physical form to an abstract idea, marking out the meridian of Paris. (*See the full description in the* Mire de Sud *section under* Sophie and Langdon's Left Bank *in the* Paving Stones of Paris *chapter.*)

Armor. This was worn by knights and noblemen. The privileges of nobility came at a price, that of protecting them for king and country in times of war. The history of armor can be traced from Homeric times to the 19th century at the Invalides Museum.

Cathars. A Christian sect that refused to acknowledge the authority of the pope. Cathars believed the cross was a symbol of human torture and disapproved of the lucrative trade of holy relics. They believed in the marriage of Christ and Mary Magdalene. The Cathars were persecuted by the Inquisition between 1209 and 1255, and they were been virtually annihilated. Little evidence of their beliefs has survived except the biased information gathered by the Inquisition. They are supposed to have hidden a great treasure, and it is suggested that this may be what Saunière found at Rennes-le-Château.

Cilice **Belt.** The *cilice* belt is a spiked band worn by certain members of Opus Dei as part of the practice known as corporal mortification. Silas wears one around his thigh. Teabing, knowing this, is able to aim for his weak spot during the moment of danger when Silas is about to steal the keystone. In Latin, the *cilicium* is a covering made of Cilician goat's hair—a horse- or goat's hair shirt was worn under fine clothing as a penance. (☞ *See also* Discipline.)

Clovis. The first Christian king of France, he was baptized at Reims on Christmas Day 496. This began the tradition of kings' being crowned there. Clovis was a Merovingian—the dynastic name comes from his grandfather Merovaeus. He died in his capital, Paris, in 511. His tomb can now be seen at the Basilica of St-Denis.

Constantine. † 337. After a vision and a military victory that he attributed to divine intervention, he converted to Christianity. He founded the Christian city of Constantinople and was one of the first builders of churches, including the Holy Sepulchre in Jerusalem. Constantine sent his mother, Helena, on a pilgrimage to seek the relics of Christ. (☞ *This story is told in a window at Ste-Chapelle; see* Ste-

Ste-Chapelle

Chapelle *in the* Paving Stones of Paris *chapter.*) St-Helena, a latecomer to Christianity, is the patron saint of people who are never on time! Constantine was baptized just before he died.

Council of Nicaea. The first ecumenical council of the church took place at Nicaea, now Iznik in Turkey, in 325 AD. The action taken at this council forms the core of *The Da Vinci Code.* Issues decided upon included the doctrine of the Holy Trinity and the divinity of Christ. The Creed of Nicaea proclaimed that Jesus and God were of the same substance—*credo* means "belief." The Creed was modified at a second council in 381. This is the Nicene Creed recited during Catholic Mass today.

Crux Ansata. This is the hooped cross used by the Coptic Church. It has the same form as the Egyptian ankh.

Crux Gemmata. This is a jewel-encrusted crucifix worn by Fache in *The Da Vinci Code.* Beautiful Visigothic examples can be seen in the Cluny Museum, suspended beneath golden votive crowns (room 16).

Dagobert. Frankish king of the Merovingian dynasty † 639. Dagobert's tomb is visible at St-Denis Basilica.

Discipline. Knotted rope used for "mortification of the flesh" by Silas in *The Da Vinci Code.* It has been used since ancient times, as has the wearing of a horsehair shirt. (☞ *See the discussion of Blaise Pascal under the* Tour St-Jacques *section of* Sophie and Langdon's Guide to Occult Paris *in the*

Paving Stones of Paris *chapter.*) Certain Opus Dei members (numeraries) use this on themselves once a week. They are encouraged to request permission to do so more often. Other forms of corporal mortification practiced by Opus Dei include sleeping on the floor with no pillow, fasting, long silences, and cold showers. The philosophy behind this is to "Chasten the body and reduce it to servitude."

> "Blessed be pain, loved be pain, sanctified be pain, glorified be pain."
>
> — *The Way*

Dossiers Secrets. This is the title of documents pertaining to the Priory of Sion, including the "Serpent Rouge." The texts were allegedly written by Henry Lobineau. Strangely, Lobineau is the name of the street just behind St-Sulpice. It is claimed that the *Dossiers Secrets* was deposited in the Bibliothèque nationale on January 17, 1967. This is the saint's day of St-Sulpice.

Et Tu, Robert? Question sent to Langdon by the Catholic bishop of Philadelphia after Langdon's TV appearance defending his Grail theory. This echoes Caesar's saying to Brutus, "Et tu, Brutus?" meaning "Even you, Brutus?" in William Shakespeare's *Julius Caesar*. Caesar says this when he realizes that Brutus is about to murder him.

Friday the 13th. Date of roundup and arrest of the Knights Templar and therefore, nowadays, associated with bad luck.

Gargoyles. The drains of churches and cathedrals, usually carved into fantastic creatures. Their name comes from the gurgling of water. There are marvellous examples at Notre-Dame, St-Merry, St-Severin, and many other churches in Paris.

Goddess Worship. Goddess worship and its suppression is a main theme of *The Da Vinci Code.* (See the Isis and the Sacred Feminine *appendix.*)

Golden Legend. This is an encyclopedia of the lives of the saints, written by medieval monk Jacques de Voragine, sometime before 1264. This book became a reference for artists, and the iconography of saints' lives is frequently based on these tales. (*See the references to Mary the Egyptian under* St-Germain l'Auxerrois *and* St-Merry *in the* Paving Stones of Paris *chapter.*)

Hermes Trismegystus. He was the teacher of a magical system known as Hermetism. High magic and alchemy were part of the schooling. Trismegystus means "three times great."

Hieros Gamos. (*See the* Isis and the Sacred Feminine *appendix.*)

Jacques de Molay. He was last of the grand masters of the Knights Templar. He's a nonfictional character, but much of his life remains a mystery.

Jesse Tree. A pictorial representation of the genealogical tree of Christ, often seen in stained glass. In Paris see Notre-Dame, Ste-Chapelle, and St-Denis Basilica; see also the Cathedral of Chartres. There is a carved Jesse Tree in Cluny. The imagery is based on the prophecy of Isaiah (11:1–3) that a Messiah would spring from the family of Jesse, father of David. Jesse is usually shown reclining with a tree growing from his loins.

Knights Templar. The story of the Knights Templar is a long and fascinating one. (*See* Sophie and Langdon's Right Bank *under their* Guide to Occult Paris *in the* Paving Stones of Paris *chapter.*)

Masons. The Masons are a society that claims ancient origins, certainly going back to medieval Masonry corporations. A document by the archbishop of Canterbury mentions the existence of Freemasons in 1396. The lodges in which they meet were originally the temporary shacks on the cathedral building sites. They employ a system of complex codes, symbols, rituals, and rites that can be understood only by the initiated. They say they are not a secret society, but that they do have secrets. To join you must be male, older than 21, have belief in a supreme being, and have no criminal record.

☞ *Many cities have Freemasonry museums—in Paris: Grand Orient de France, 16 rue Cadet, 75009, metro Cadet or Grands-Boulevards (see map, p. 35), open 2–6pm Tuesday–Saturday.*

Meridian. Meridian means "midday." At any location, it is the arc on the earth at right angles to the Equator passing from North to South poles. All celestial objects reach their highest point in the sky here—the sun is on the meridian at local noon. To create your own local meridian, choose the spot you wish the meridian to pass through, stick a pole in the spot, and verify its verticality. Trace a perfect circle around the pole. The circumference will be that of the length of the shadow cast by the pole at a chosen time, say 10am. Mark the spot with an A. Watch the shadow during the course of the day and mark the circle exactly at the moment when the shadow falls on the opposite side. Mark point B. Join the points A and B with a line, and divide the line in half. Mark point C. The meridian is the line running from the foot of your pole through point C. You can now build your own gnomon.

Merovingians. This ancient dynasty of Frankish kings died out in 751. The last Merovingian was Theoderic IV, and his son Childeric III was deposed. In France, these kings are known as the *rois fainéants*, or the Do-Little Kings. *The Da Vinci Code* story is based on the claim that this dynasty was descended from the union of Christ and Mary Magdalene.

Mire du Nord/Sud. These are the north and south markers of the Paris Meridian. (☞ *See the descriptions under* Sophie and Langdon's Guide to Occult Paris *in the* Paving Stones of Paris *chapter.*)

Opus Dei. A little-publicized group till the advent of *The Da Vinci Code*, it was founded by a Spaniard, Josemaria Escriva de Balaguer, in 1928. Pope John Paul II gave independence and status to the church by making it a personal prelature in 1982. A personal prelature is a jurisdictional entity within the Catholic Church's own hierarchical structure. The pope also beatified Escriva in 2002. Apparently there are about

80,000 members worldwide. The organization has been criticized for its recruitment techniques, often aiming at the young and the emotionally fragile. Numerary members generally live in Opus Dei houses, vow celibacy, practice corporal mortification with *cilice* and discipline (this is Silas), and have every aspect of their lives controlled; for example, contact with family is discouraged. Most give a large part, if not all, of their salaries to the organization. Dan Brown includes the Opus Dei Watch Dog website in his book; www.odan.org makes gloomy but fascinating reading.

Phi. (☞ *See* Sophie Neveu *under* Sophie's World *in this appendix.*)

Philosopher's Stone. Metaphorical in alchemy, like the sword in the stone, it probably symbolizes "that which contains unobtainable knowledge." The stone also refers to the raw materials that make the elixir that allows for the transformation of base metals into gold. A carved fountain at the Museum of Arts and Metiers shows a low-relief ship symbolizing alchemy; the stone is to the right of the mast.

Priory of Sion. (☞ *See* Sophie and Langdon's Guide to Occult Paris *in the* Paving Stones of Paris *chapter and the* Story of St-Sulpice *in the* Beneath the Rose Line *chapter; also see* Knights Templar *in the index.*)

☞ *To discover more about this intriguing secret society, join a Paris Walks Da Vinci Code guided tour, noon on Saturdays, tel. 01/48-09-21-40.*

SmartCar. Sophie drives a fashionable SmartCar, very handy for parking in Paris and quite a speedy getaway vehicle, although not much room for storing loot. The car was originally developed

as a joint venture between Swatch and Mercedes-Benz in 1994. The prototype was to be electric but after difficulties, the gasoline version was launched. (The car is made by Daimler Chrysler at Smartville, at Hambach in Lorraine, France.) Each one takes eight hours to make; that is about one foot per hour. The standard French model is called the "fortwo." The model being launched for America is an SUV and called the "formore" (only for those who have a "fortune").

Tarot. Brown mentions Tarot and the pack's suit of pentacles. In France the most traditional pack is made by Grimaud and is called the Tarot de Marseilles. The cards are used for a game as well as fortune-telling. There is no suit of pentacles in the traditional French pack, which consists of coins, batons, cups, and swords. Some versions, including the attractive arts and crafts Rider Waite pack, do. Tarot is believed to date to about 1450. The original imagery was Christian, but in the 17th century the pack was influenced by alchemy and astrology. The Marseilles Tarot dates from 1760. The card illustrated shows a goddess figure surrounded by the tetramorph, and it is titled "the world," perhaps as the feminine aspect of God.

Tetramorph. The four symbols of the evangelists have their origins in the book of Revelation. A winged man is Matthew, a lion is Mark, an eagle is John, and the ox is Luke. This symbolism can be seen on many churches; one of the most beautiful tetramorphs is at Chartres. In Paris one can be seen on the pulpit of St-Gervais–St-Protais Church.

Wicca. This is a modern association of white witches. The witch, earth mother, nurturer, and healer, was violently suppressed by the church, especially during the 16th and 17th

tetramorph at Chartres

centuries. Academics propose differing numbers of how many were executed or burned. It is generally accepted that during about 12,000 trials, 40,000–60,000 were executed. Langdon says about five million as he tells of Saunière's personal passion for Wicca.

The Codes

Anagrams. Probably used by the ancient Greeks, and by the medieval period were attributed with mystical power. Dan Brown's book is riddled with anagrams; they are supposed to reveal what is in a name: Wolfgang Amadeus Mozart equals A Famous German Waltz God. Dan Brown says the Romans referred to anagrams as Ars Magna, the "Great Art," but this is just another clever anagram of the word "anagrams."

Atbash Cipher. Extremely ancient code. A simple substitution cipher in which the first letter of the alphabet is replaced with the last, the second with the second to last, and so on, till the alphabet is completely reversed—in other words, A is coded as Z, B coded as Y, C coded as X. The name Atbash is based upon the substitution itself. It is made up by pronouncing the first, last, second, and second to last syllables of the Hebrew alphabet. This cipher is used in the Bible; in Jeremiah 25:26, Sheshach becomes Babel. Hugh Schonfield applied this to the name of Baphomet and found it made Sophia. (☞ *See* Baphomet *under* Langdon's Dictionary of Symbols, Sacred and Profane *in the* Seven Seals *appendix.*)

Baconian. In chapter 20 of *The Da Vinci Code*, Langdon remembers his work on Baconian manuscripts. The 13th-century English monk Roger Bacon wrote *Epistle on the Secret Works of Art and Nobility of Magic*. This is the first known European book to discuss cryptography. By the next century ciphers were in common use by alchemists and scientists as a means of concealing their findings. Bacon presented seven different methods for coding texts.

Caesar Cipher. Used by Caesar and by Dan Brown on the front cover of the first edition of his book. In the computer age this is an easy cipher to crack. The letters in the alphabet are shifted by a given number. This is similar to Atbash but there is no reversal, just a shifting. If the given number is three, then C becomes A, D becomes B, E becomes C, and so on. As E is the most common letter used, a message can be decrypted by working out the most common letter, equating it to E, and then working out the given shift.

Da Vinci. He wrote many of his texts in mirror writing. This did not give high-security protection to his ideas, but at a time when many were illiterate it would have made it hard for anyone looking over his shoulder to see what he was writing. He was left-handed, which would have made mirror writing practical in the days when ink took time to dry. It is far easier for left-handed than right-handed people to write in this fashion, although it takes practice.

Drosnin, Michael. Wrote *The Bible Code*. Having made contact with the mathematician Dr. Eliyahu Rips, Drosnin exposed the theory that the Bible encoded predictions. He was so entirely convinced that there was a system of codes, he warned Yitzhak Rabin of the prediction of his assassination. Some months later the prediction proved to come true. The work has been derided by many, but despite this, some of the predictions have proved true.

Fibonacci Sequence. (☞ *See* Golden Numbers *under* Exterior of the Church *in the* Beneath the Rose Line *chapter.*)

Jefferson's Wheel Cipher. Around 1800, Thomas Jefferson invented his Wheel Cipher. This consists of rings containing the letters of the alphabet. Each ring can turn around a central axis. As long as your correspondent has the same setup, he can decode your messages.

Palindrome. A word that reads the same backward as forward, for example "wow" or "mom," or a phrase such as "A Toyota's a Toyota!" or "Cain a maniac," or, just perfect for *The Da Vinci Code*, "Madam, in Eden I'm Adam."

The Templars' Code. The Knights Templar had a secret code that they used to protect their promissory notes and documents. It was based upon placing the letters of the alphabet around their emblem, the vermillion cross. This is very much like the modern "Pig Pen Code".

Vatican. The Vatican has used a secret code for centuries. It remains secret!

Paris and Its Grand Masters of the Priory of Sion

Between 1188 and 1963, 26 men are listed as having been grand masters of the Priory of Sion. Some of these have been particularly influential in Paris. Notably:

Nicolas Flamel, grand master 1398–1418. Well known for his involvement in alchemy, wealthy benefactor of Parisian institutions. Was buried at the church of St-Jacques-de-la-Boucherie in Paris. (☞ *See* Sophie and Langdon's Right Bank *under* Sophie and Langdon's Guide to Occult Paris *in the* Paving Stones of Paris *chapter; also see the* Cluny Museum of Medieval Art *under* Sophie and Langdon's Left Bank *in the same chapter.*)

Leonardo da Vinci, grand master 1510–1519. Not especially influential in Paris, but he had huge influence on France's King Francis I. It was to Francis that da Vinci bequeathed the *Mona Lisa*. Francis I was a kind and generous patron, providing for the artist and asking only the pleasure of his conversation and ideas in return. Da Vinci died in the beautiful Château of Clos-Lucé in Amboise. (☞ *For a life of da Vinci, see the* Under the Pyramids *chapter.*)

Connetable de Bourbon, grand master 1519–1527. Enemy of Francis I, he was put on trial in his absence and found guilty of *lèse-majesté*, rebellion, and felony. His lands and possessions were confiscated. His arms were effaced, he was deprived of the name Bourbon, and the door of his Paris town house was painted yellow, a symbol of his fall from grace. Bourbon won the respect of the imperial army, which was in a mood of murderous mutiny, having been unpaid for months. He promised to make them rich by sacking Rome. In fact, he attacked the pope in the castle of Sant'Angelo. The mystery of just what he was looking for remains to be answered.

Victor Hugo, grand master 1844–1885. Much of his life was spent in Paris, but there were periods of exile during the reign of Napoleon III. In Paris, an avenue is named after him, and he lived there for a short while, his address being M. Victor Hugo, in this avenue, Paris! (☞ *For more on Hugo, see* Sophie and Langdon's Right Bank *under* Sophie and Langdon's Guide to Occult Paris *in the* Paving Stones of Paris *chapter.*)

Claude Debussy, grand master 1885–1918. Musician and composer who won the Rome Prize for Music at age 22. He is described as a brilliant but rebellious student. His early music lessons were taken with Mme Mauté de Fleurville, student of Frédéric Chopin and mother-in-law of Paul Verlaine, who had much influence on his work. In the 1880s, Debussy frequented the symbolist poets and lived the bohemian life of an artist in Montmartre.

☞ *You can visit the apartment where he was born; it's above the tourist office (at one time his parents' shop) in St-Germain-en-Laye.*

Jean Cocteau, grand master 1918–1963. Immensely influential in the world of the arts. Brilliant draftsman, painter, poet, and filmmaker. Discretely influential everywhere. Cocteau was passionate about secrets and created a whole world of symbols in which he lived his life. He was very influenced by religion, surrealism, psychoanalysis, and cubism, and he loved ceremony and ritual. He became a member of many important organizations. In 1949, he became a chevalier of the Legion of Honor and in 1955, a member of the Académie francaise. At the Académie he had access to two libraries containing nearly two million ancient documents, manuscripts, alchemical works, and some of the most creatively mysterious works of da Vinci!

APPENDIX 3:

ISIS
AND THE
SACRED
FEMININE

THIS SECTION explains some of the theory on which *The Da Vinci Code* is based. It examines some of the historical sources and indicates where appropriate examples can be seen in Paris.

Among the many fascinating but controversial themes explored by *The Da Vinci Code* is that of the "sacred feminine." This theme is the central core of the story, and two of its heroes, Langdon and the Louvre curator, Saunière, are specialists in this field of study. We learn that Langdon has spent much of the previous year writing a book about the symbols and art associated with goddess worship. The title of his book is *Symbols of the Lost Sacred Feminine*. This is also Saunière's primary area of expertise. We are told that he is "the premiere goddess iconographer on earth" and that his contribution to the Louvre is "the largest collection of goddess art on earth." (☞ *The relevant collection is described in detail in the Louvre chapter,* Under the Pyramids.)

When Sophie Neveu and Langdon arrive at Château Villette, the first thing they notice is a statue of Isis on Teabing's mantelpiece. This ancient goddess symbolizes his devotion to the subject. The importance of Isis and her relationship to Paris will shortly be explained.

THE SACRED FEMININE ELIMINATED BY THE CHURCH

The Da Vinci Code is about rival groups and their quest for the Holy Grail. When Teabing explains the Grail as a concept to Sophie, he says that most people want to know where it is, but he argues that the most important question is, "What it is." He goes on to explain that the Grail is in fact the relics of the ultimate sacred feminine, Mary Magdalene. Teabing has dedicated his life to the study of this and the evidence he uses as proof of his discovery is the codes he sees encrypted by da Vinci in his paintings.

Mary and Christ *by Pigalle (St-Sulpice) R.R.*

DEAD SEA SCROLLS AND NAG HAMMADI TEXTS

These arguments are not a fabrication of Dan Brown's but are based upon long-standing academic study. They are in part built upon the ancient Coptic codices found at Nag Hammadi in Egypt in 1945 and the Dead Sea Scrolls found at Qumran in the 1950s. Teabing argues that the significance of these texts is that they were written long before the council of Nicaea in 325 AD, when the texts to be included in the Bible were chosen. These rediscovered texts reveal things about Christ, such as his life and ministry, that were well known but purposefully excluded from the Bible.

TRANSMOGRIFICATION

Religious scholars argue that the rise of the church was more than in part due to the need for political unification: One king and one god had to be a more stable system than that of countless pagan religions that divided people. As the church developed, it adopted and then adapted important pagan rites and symbols, and slowly but surely these transmogrified into

Where to Find the Lost Sacred Feminine in Paris

Carnavalet Museum

Carnavalet Museum (history of Paris), 23 rue de Sévigné, 75004, metro St-Paul (see map, p. 53), open 10am–6pm, closed Mondays.

Cluny Museum (Gallo–Roman and medieval Paris), 6 place Paul-Painlevé, 75005, metro Cluny-la-Sorbonne (see map, p. 79), closed Tuesdays.

Louvre Museum, 75001, metro Palais-Royal-Musée-du-Louvre (see map, p. 21), closed Tuesdays. (☞ *See also* Isis and the Egyptians *in the* Antiquities *section of the* Under the Pyramids *chapter.*)

Museum of Eroticism (the author hasn't been there!), 72 boulevard de Clichy, 75018, metro Blanche (see map, p. 35), open 10am–2pm every day.

St-Germain-en-Laye (prehistory to Merovingians), place du Château, 78100 Saint-Germain-en-Laye, RER St-Germain-en-Laye, closed Tuesdays.

Nos Ancêtres les Gaulois/Our Gallic Ancestors (worshipers of Isis), rue St-Louis-en-l'Île (see map, p. 53), is a lively restaurant on Île St-Louis and great fun for parties.

a new system of culture and belief. Langdon gives several examples: Images of Isis with her miraculously concieved son, Horus, became the model for later representations of the Virgin Mary and Child, and the halos of saints were based upon the sun disks of Egyptian gods and goddesses. Evidence of this can be seen in the Louvre collections. The veneration of the sacred feminine seems to have traveled through the Middle East, the Indus Valley, the Mediterranean, and then through Europe in general. There is a statue of Isis–Aphrodite in the Louvre. As the church became the dominant force, goddess worship was pushed underground. The church subverted the role of its holiest women and Mary Magdalene was misrepresented as a prostitute. At Nicaea the Virgin Mary became the Theotokos, or mother of God, and was given a submissive role. The doctrine confirming her own birth by immaculate conception and her infant's virgin birth can be seen as distancing her from the pagan image of fertility goddesses and human intervention in procreation. God, priest, king, and father would soon replace goddess, queen, priestess, and mother. Langdon says that the Grail is an ancient symbol of womanhood that has been lost, eliminated by the church.

GODDESS WORSHIP IN PREHISTORIC TIMES

There is plenty of evidence that goddess worship is among man's most ancient activities. Statuettes and figurines representing the sacred feminine date back thousands of years. Some beautiful examples can be seen in the Carnavalet Museum in Paris. An exceptional figurine in pottery was recently found during the excavations of the prehistoric settlement at Bercy on the eastern  side of Paris. The Bercy figurine, dated at around 4,000 BC, is made of clay, and she represents a female form with her hands resting on her belly. She is very obviously a representation of

The Hooded Woman, *21,000 BC*   *statuette, 23,000 BC*

female fertility. Other examples of ancient female statuettes can be seen at the museum of St-Germain-en-Laye, just outside Paris. In the museum is a collection of stone figurines that are among the most ancient known, dating from about 23,000 BC. The collection includes one of the earliest and most beautiful representations to be carved with facial features; it's known as the *Dame à la Capuche* (*The Hooded Woman*) and comes from Brassempouy in the Landes region. It is dated to about 21,000 BC. The Romans also made figurines of mother goddesses; many of these are shown suckling a child on each breast. The figurines, mostly ceramic, were mass-produced. Both the molds for manufacturing, and the figurines themselves, can be seen in the above-mentioned museums.

FERTILITY

For ancient man, reproduction and agriculture were the vital elements of his survival. The fertility of crops, animals, and the human race were seen as divine and mysterious. The powerful act of procreation was also considered as mystical and therefore venerated. Procreation was miraculous and benificent, and it therefore could only be the work of God. The symbolism of these pagan rites was often simple and unambiguous, such as the dancing in circles around the May Pole in spring. The culmination of this basic belief was a sexual rite symbolizing a sacred marriage.

HIEROS GAMOS

This rite was practiced by various ancient civilizations, including the Sumerians, Greeks, Romans, and Celtic Druids. A reenactment of this was unwittingly witnessed by the young Sophie Neveu in her grandfather's house. At this point, she realizes that he must be a member of a secret sect. The ceremony of Hieros Gamos is explained to Sophie by Teabing and Langdon as they escape to London in Teabing's private jet. When Sophie finally admits that she actually witnessed this strange and frightening event, Langdon explains that Hieros Gamos actually means "Sacred Marriage," a spiritual union through which male and female experience God. Langdon goes on to explain that the rite has been used for more than 2,000 years, since the ancient Egyptians initially venerated Isis. The unfortunate witnessing of this ceremony, which revolts and frightens Sophie, leads her to cut all ties with her grandfather. This family rift is irreconcilable despite Saunière's many attempts to contact Sophie.

Langdon makes it clear that what happened is evidence of the Priory of Sion's celebration of the sacred feminine. The idea of physical union as sacred has existed since ancient times. Examples of this can be seen in the Tantric rites of Hindu Yogis. There are also plenty of examples of the bridge between eroticism and spirituality in the décor of ancient Hindu temples, for ex-

ample the 13th-century Sun Temple of Konarak, in the Bay of Bengal region of Orissa. Shakti is the divine sexual aspect of Kali Ma, the dark goddess of destruction and creation. The lingam is a small altar or shrine that symbolizes the vulva and the phallus united. The shop windows of the passage Brady, in Paris's Indian quarter, are full of these images and symbols.

☞ To visit passage Brady and the Indian quarter, go to metro Château-d'Eau or walk along the rue du Faubourg-St-Denis northward from the gare du Nord (see map, p. 35).

Hermaphrodite to Adam

An example of Hieros Gamos exists in an ancient Sumerian poem about 5,000 years old. It describes the ceremony taking place between a priestess called Innana and King Dumuzi. The union of the priestess with the king in the temple celebrates the goddess's acceptance of the king as ruler of her people and reinforces the divinity associated with the role of king. A Sophian Gnostic tract says that Adam is in a state of Hieros Gamos at the outset, being both male and female, like Hermaphrodite, until the creation of Eve. Dan Brown includes this ceremony to emphasize that it is the church that gives the label "original sin" to what was previously seen as the divine mystery of procreation.

From Sacred Marriage to Christ's Marriage

Dan Brown's book makes it clear that goddess worship and the notion of the sacred feminine have been inherent in humankind's psyche since its origins. The book goes further by emphasizing the following argument: The sacred feminine was so important that eventually Christ would trust the continuation of the church to a woman, this being Mary Magdalene, to whom, according to this theory, Christ was married. The principal argument used by those who follow this belief is based upon the content of ancient texts among the Dead Sea Scrolls, and two particular extracts from the Nag Hammadi texts.

From the Gnostic Gospels' "Gospel of Philip"

"And the companion of the Saviour is Mary Magdalene." In the same gospel appears the passage: "But Christ loved [Mary Magdalene] more than all the disciples and used to kiss her often on the mouth. The rest of the disciples were offended by it and expressed disapproval. They said to him, 'Why do you love her more than all of us?'"

In biblical times, kissing on the mouth was purportedly the reserve of married couples alone. The original Greek word "companion" meant "consort" or "married partner." Grail scholars have of course made much of this.

CHRIST'S BLOODLINE

The Da Vinci Code argues that the church has been fighting ever since its origins to maintain its male domination, and that it has made every effort possible to cover up this ancient truth. It is argued that the very reason that these texts were hidden at Nag Hammadi is that they were already seen as heretical by the church in the very early Christian era. This fact, Brown argues, has been understood by an elite of small groups or sects. These have struggled in the form of secret societies, using their codes, artwork, and symbols to pass on the message of the importance of the sacred feminine. The Christian ideal of the sacred feminine is encapsulated in the notion of the Holy Grail. This consists of both the physical relics of Mary Magdalene and certain documents concerning her life and her role. Teabing tells us not only that Leonardo da Vinci was one of the keepers of the secret, but that he headed a secret society, the Priory of Sion, whose purpose was to protect the secret and the descendants of Christ and Mary Magdalene. The secret is of course purported to be preserved for future generations in a complex series of cryptic clues in the artist's paintings. These clues are fully explained in the descriptions of his works. The descendants of Christ and Mary Magdalene, Dan Brown tells us, were the Merovingians: a powerful dynasty of Frankish kings who made Paris their capital.

BACK TO ISIS

It is said that Paris owes its name to the sacred feminine, Isis. For the Egyptians, the name of Isis meant "throne" or "seat," and it was therefore of special significance to the ruler. If there is truth in Dan Brown's tale, it would be fitting and logical that Isis was chosen to symbolize the capital of the Merovingians. Ancient texts show a temple dedicated to Isis in the St-Germain-des-Prés area. A Gallo–Roman shrine to the goddess is recorded at the foothill of Montmartre, named Lucotèce in ancient times. Isis also has figured on the coat of arms of the city, which can be seen today on a school building in the Marais, on rue Vieille-du-Temple. An ancient statue of Isis was kept in St-Germain-des-Prés

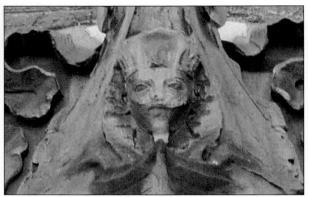

Isis, rue Vieille-du-Temple

Church, and it is described in a book called *La Fleur des antiquités de Paris (The Most Beautiful Parisian Antiquities)*, published in 1561. The abbot of St-Germain, Guillaume Briçonet, had the statue smashed in the 16th century. The lost sacred feminine of Paris was never to be replaced. By the time Isis had come to the Greeks, she had become the protector of seamen and received a rudder as her attribute. The founders of Paris, the Parisii, were a powerful nautical guild who had a galleon as their emblem, and it is possibly because of this that Isis, their protector, became the emblem of Paris. Carvings of the founders of Paris and their nautical guild can be seen on the magnificent Gallo–Roman pillar excavated from beneath the nave of Notre-Dame. This is now kept in the Cluny Museum of Paris.

Index

Acknowledgments

No book is written without the help of more people than it is possible to mention.

Special thanks go to Constance de Bartillat and Charles Ficat for the initial idea, and their energy, encouragement, and enthusiasm. Mike at Village Voice for the "Priory" inside story. Marcio for keeping the computers going. The team of guides for keeping Paris Walks going while I was busy researching. Oriel, my wife, for research, proofreading, corrections, and putting up with it all. Thanks also to my family and friends for their encouragement and enthusiasm, and finally to all our clients for whom this guide is written.

Photo Credits

Illustrations on pages 3, 17, 87, 109, 135, 151, 159, 175
© 2006 Jupiterimages Corporation

Photos on pages 16–17, 61, 150–151, 158–159, 174–175, 187, 198–199 © Phil Shipman
page 27 © Susannah Sayler
pages 86–87 © Digital Archive Japan / Alamy
page 128 © Gianni Dagli Orti / CORBIS
page 130 © Erich Lessing / Art Resource, NY
pages 134–135 © Martial Colomb / Getty Images
Chateau de Villette by permission
page 176, Cryptex by Justin Nevins

All other photos © Peter Caines. Other documents and objects from the author's collection.

PARIS WALKS
Discover Paris on our Walking Tours

Paris Walks is a small company, founded in 1994, which offers a great variety of tours in Paris that explore neighborhoods, themes, or museums.

The tours run all year, and you can join us on a scheduled walk or book our excellent guides for a private tour. We have a small team of guides, who are mostly British or American, but who have lived in Paris for many years and enjoy sharing their love of the city with our clients. The tours are well researched and informative, but also lively and enjoyable. If you come on one of our tours, you will always see a mixture of famous places and lesser-known charming details. A tour led by an enthusiastic guide sharing a love of Paris with the group is the perfect complement to this book.

Our schedule of tours each month can be found on our website, www.paris-walks.com. Regular tours include the beautiful historic districts of the city: the Marais, Montmartre, the Latin Quarter, St-Germain, Île de la Cité. We have thematic visits such as Hemingway's Paris, the French Revolution, and the Occupation. We also offer tours of other places of interest: Père Lachaise Cemetery, the Paris Opera House, the Sewers, the Catacombs, the Conciergerie Prison. For those who live in Paris, we have courses to follow French history and art in the many beautiful Paris museums.

OUR WALKING TOUR ON THE THEME OF PARIS AND *THE DA VINCI CODE* TAKES PLACE EVERY SATURDAY AT 10:30AM.

CONTACT US FOR MORE DETAILS:
TEL: 01/48-09-21-40
FROM ABROAD: 33-1/48-09-21-40
E-MAIL: PARIS@PARIS-WALKS.COM
OR LOOK AT THE CURRENT SCHEDULE
AT WWW.PARIS-WALKS.COM

Walking the Da Vinci Code in Paris
First U.S. Edition Avalon Travel Publishing 2006

Avalon Travel Publishing
An Imprint of
Avalon Publishing Group, Inc.

1400 65th Street, Suite 250
Emeryville, CA 94608, USA
atpfeedback@avalonpub.com
www.travelmatters.com

Editor: Grace Fujimoto
Design: Gerilyn Attebery
Copy Editor: Karen Gaynor Bleske
Graphics Coordinator: Stefano Boni
Production Coordinator: Darren Alessi
Map Editor: Kat Smith
Cartographers: Mike Morgenfeld, Kat Bennett, Suzanne Service
Indexer: Karen Gaynor Bleske

ISBN-10: 1-59880-044-2
ISBN-13: 978-1-59880-044-9
ISSN: 1559-8853

Printing History
1st edition—April 2006
5 4 3 2 1